Kicking
the
Habit

Kicking the Habit

the Autobiography of England's
Most Infamous Football Hooligan

Jason Marriner

Fort Publishing Ltd

First published in 2015 by Fort Publishing Ltd, Old Belmont House, 12 Robsland Avenue, Ayr, KA7 2RW

Printed by Bell and Bain Ltd, Glasgow

Typeset by 3btype.com

Graphic design by Mark Blackadder

Front-cover photograph by Simon Harsent

ISBN: 978-1905769-47-6

*I dedicate this book to every
man and woman in the armed forces.
They are the real heroes, 365 days a year.*

Contents

Preface

I have been asked to write this book on numerous occasions. After being arrested in 2010 for Cardiff and sent down again, I thought, 'fuck it, why not?' It's the end of the road for me in the scene, or at least that's what I tell myself.

If you're looking for 'We've never been done' and 'We've never been run' this is the wrong book for you. If you want truthfulness and humour then I'm sure this book is a bit of you.

You can't please everyone and everyone's a critic. We all see things differently. But I've been as honest as I can. There are a lot of jealous and sore people out there amongst a lot of haters. The people who dislike me are the people who generally don't know me. The love and support I get is overwhelming. So from the bottom of my heart I thank you, as I'm just a normal kid who comes from the street.

I am afraid to say that whether you're in the public eye or not, people will start rumours and talk shit about you. The truth of it is, they are lies. But I'm afraid that's drink and drugs for you. We've all heard rumours that are embarrassing and cringe-worthy. I haven't got the time to listen to people's bollocks. But I am afraid there will always be gossip-mongers who have nothing better to do.

I am currently in talks with the youngest British film producer, a man with his finger on the pulse. He knows what the public wants to see. His name is Jonathan Sothcott.

So to my headmaster, schoolteachers, the lollipop man and dinner ladies, who all said I wouldn't do anything with my life, I'd like to say one thing.

'Fuck you.'

But thanks for your opinion.

Jason Marriner
April 2015

Prologue: A Setup

I was where I wanted to be. No that's wrong. I was where I had to be: on the streets around my beloved Stamford Bridge, ready to see off cunts who had come to London with mayhem on their minds. It was 13 February 2010, the fifth round of the FA Cup, a lunchtime kickoff. The Cardiff Soul Crew were in town, desperate to put one over on the Chelsea Headhunters.

That was never going to happen.

No one, but no one, comes here and takes liberties with the best mob this country has ever produced. Another English firm doing it is bad enough but to let the Welsh take the piss would have been a severe blow to national pride.

You will say I was crazy. This was after MacIntyre, a little episode that had got me a six stretch, however undeserved the sentence. After a quarter of a century on the scene, I was now forty-three years old, a Category C hooligan, with more form than Red Rum. Given my record a conviction would definitely see me put behind the door again, at a time of life when doing bird is even harder. The older you get the harder it is. I was one of the best-known faces in the land, which is nothing to be proud of but it's the truth and a fact. So what with the new technology, specialist football-intelligence units, internet keyboard warriors and grasses the chances were that I would be standing in the dock again in front of the old chocolate fudge.

'Why didn't you just stay away?'

I wish I had a pound for every time I have been asked that question.

My answer? Addiction.

It is a logical question. But I have never been guided by logic. I even got nicked at a Chelsea–West Ham game the day after I came off my ten-year ban and was charged with a public-order offence. Although I wasn't convicted, it was enough to get me another football ban.

So here I was again, risking it all.

And for what? My addiction.

For the raw surge of energy that football violence gives you, a more powerful high than drinks, drugs and sex combined. Many lads will tell you that football violence is an addiction and while that is certainly true, for me it was more, much more. It was a way of life, steaming in, standing your ground no matter what was in front of you, backing up your mates, being part of something.

From the 1970s onwards Chelsea's mob has wreaked havoc at home and abroad. In September 1983 three hundred Chelsea faces went down to Brighton and fucking wrecked the place; and by *place* I mean both the Goldstone ground and the town. Brighton chairman Mike Bamber said it was the worst violence he had ever seen. It was a great day out at the seaside; three lads got cut including one who, according to the local Brighton paper, 'was slashed from shoulder to hip with a Stanley knife'. Dozens were hospitalised, among them, I am pleased to say, several of Brighton's Old Bill. The next day a cache of petrol bombs was discovered up an alley; that would have been spectacular but, as *The Sun* noted, the find was made 'mercifully before they could be used'.

That was us all over in those days. A year after Brighton, in October 1984, we kicked off at the Dell, resulting in Southampton banning us from their ground. We put the fear of God into everyone: in 1982 the *Daily Mirror* reported that Tottenham had returned a thousand tickets for an FA Cup quarter final at the Bridge because . . . well, the clue is in there. As Mike Pouncett, their ticket-office manager, explained: 'A few of our regulars said there was no way they would go to Chelsea. They gave me the clear impression they were frightened.' You and I both know the papers talk bollocks but we were on a mission.

One of our best days was at Derby, at the old Baseball Ground. When they scored late on in the game to knock us out of the FA Cup we lost the plot. The place got smashed to bits. Chelsea started a fire, threw seats onto the pitch and pelted any cunt within reach with bottles and coins. I have been to a million-and-one games but for whatever reason we talk about Derby to this day. There will always be favourites and that was one of mine.

That little altercation led to our fans being temporarily banned from away games and to even more angry editorials in national newspapers, some of which demanded that Chelsea should be thrown out of football. After reading the papers, T-shirts with the logo 'You can't ban a Chelsea fan' started to appear.

We spawned so many legends of football violence in those golden years. Many were with us for Cardiff; some could not make it due to bans or because they had retired from the scene. My thoughts drifted back to the early Eighties when, in my early teens, I met the man who would become not only my mentor but also a very good friend: Steve 'Hickey' Hickmott. Hickey did more than anyone else to create the fighting machine that became the Headhunters. He was a brilliant, and tireless, organiser, an inspiration to us all, as game as fuck with a good personality.

He wasn't from the usual hooligan background. He was a middle-class boy from Tunbridge Wells, that bastion of Middle England, synonymous with retired colonels, tea with the vicar and readers of the *Daily Telegraph*. Not surprisingly, he was very well-spoken.

'We have come for an altercation,' he would proclaim in that snobby accent of his.

Then when it went off he would always be one of the front runners, the posh kid kicking and punching his way through enemy lines.

We couldn't let him down. Nor the many others we had stood with throughout the golden years of the Seventies and Eighties.

From the moment the draw was made the phone never stopped. We were so excited. I know Cardiff felt the same way; after all, it wasn't just two clubs meeting – it was England versus Wales, with all the historical baggage that goes with it. I knew that blokes who never went near the football would be on the bus; to take on Chelsea was a story they could tell their grandkids. And with Cardiff getting an allocation of six thousand tickets they were going to have one hell of a mob with them.

Our plan was to avoid meeting in the pub, where the cozzers could corral us, and to be out on the street early, terrorising them. That's what they would have done to us. Cardiff are used to taking big numbers with them, throwing their weight around, intimidating the locals. Not this time, not in our backyard.

Just as we had planned it the Fulham Road was buzzing nice and early, with hundreds of Chelsea lads around, all well up for it. The violence started first thing in the morning, as soon as the Welsh got to London. This was confirmed by *The Sun*, which later reported that 'more than 100 Chelsea yobs marched on North End Road, splitting into two groups with military precision to attack Cardiff coaches'.

I got there at half-nine, and took a call saying we had spotters out in Hammersmith to find out where the Welsh were drinking. It soon got back to us: Cardiff were in the George. Before long, one of the Taffs called me. He was keen to get the ball rolling.

'We're in Hammersmith. Are you lot going to come over here?'

I laughed down the phone. 'You're playing Chelsea you cunt, not QPR. Get on the Oxo, get off at West Brompton and we'll meet you in the graveyard behind the ground.'

I wasn't among the group who went to the graveyard. It was mainly our Youth, who had become very impatient. But it went off big time there, as it later did over the whole area. By this time the tension was overwhelming. We knew something big was in the air.

The scene that day would have gladdened the heart of any lad worth his salt. Big mobs of Chelsea and Cardiff were milling around, looking for a way to get at each other; urging the other lot to fight, eager to strike the first blow. Meanwhile, seventy of our boys, all on banning orders, were stuck in a pub in Tooting Bec, outside the banning perimeter, desperate to get into the action but unable to get amongst it. The Old Bill were starting to panic, but being very aggressive at the same time. To be fair the tension was running high. They knew something was going to happen and they wanted to stamp their authority as quickly as possible.

We didn't need any extra incentive to attack the Soul Crew and their hangers-on. The fixture was more than enough.

But they gave us one anyway.

We were on the Fulham Road when a Cardiff lad spat at Blind Jerry, a Chelsea fan who had been going to the Bridge for as long as I can remember (sadly, Jerry has now passed away). The cunt must have known Jerry was blind. He had a guide dog for fuck's sake.

The red mist descended. We steamed in, our anger leaving the Old Bill helpless. Fights erupted all over the place until police on horseback arrived and split us up. Cardiff were pushed to one side of the road while we were on the other. It didn't work because, as we were being driven up the street, skirmishes were taking place all over the gaff. I don't know if it's something Cardiff do everywhere, but they started chanting 'Soul Crew, Soul Crew'. I pissed myself laughing. We had never chanted 'Headhunters, Headhunters' in our lives. Maybe we were meant to be scared.

Like the rest of our front runners I was trying my best to get at Cardiff but the Old Bill were doing their utmost to keep us away. Other cozzers decided that it would be a good idea to do some steaming-in of their own and lashed out at both mobs with their truncheons. In the scuffles that followed one cozzer got a broken jaw and four teeth knocked out after being hit in the face with a rock. Meanwhile one of our boys was bitten on the arm by a police dog.

With the numbers on both sides in the several hundreds the Old Bill realised that the situation had the potential to turn even nastier and now their only priority was to get both mobs into the ground, which they eventually succeeded in doing.

At the end of the game I got the shock of my life. When I got out of the ground I realised that the police had let the six thousand Cardiff out at the same time as us. Surely they must have known it would create the potential for a riot. I understand times have changed and supporters are let out at the same time but not when the opposition has been given six thousand tickets and there has been continuous fighting in the hours leading up to the game, one that was classified as a Category C fixture. Looking back at it now it wasn't a schoolboy error by the Old Bill. This was a clever move to see how many banning orders they could give out. They gave us the rope and we hung ourselves.

By the time I reached the forecourt it was pandemonium. The street was chock-a-block with Cardiff, Chelsea and Old Bill. Within seconds it had gone off, with everyone swinging punches. We noticed that, not content with taking on the Headhunters, Cardiff were picking on Chelsea scarfers, who, it has to be said, were giving a good account of themselves.

We decided to go down Holmead Road, which leads towards the King's Road. Meanwhile, about a hundred and fifty Cardiff had gone down an alley with the intention of mobbing up and attacking us whenever they could dodge police lines. Normally, that alley was blocked off by uniformed units but today it was clear. Another change to police procedures, which to me was very suspicious indeed.

I was at the front of our mob beside Billy Matthews, with the rest of our lads just behind us. Cardiff's front runners had already picked off some normal bods on the King's Road. Then they saw us running towards them. I noticed that a Chelsea scarfer had been having a row with a fat Welsh cunt and had put him on the floor. I had a split-second in which to decide whether to volley the cunt or drop him out. I decided to leave him alone as the scarfer had done himself proud.

The two mobs came face to face. The Battle of the King's Road was about to begin.

When they saw how many of us there were they were taken aback.

They backed off and pelted us with bricks, bottles and even workmen's signs that they had dug out of a skip. One of their front runners charged into us head first but his suicide mission turned out to be just that as he took a hell of a beating. Their missile-lobbing tactic could only work while they had ammunition. When they ran out it was our turn. The normal bouncing up and down started and an almighty roar went up.

We ran them and it was undoubtedly a great victory but as they backed off, a lot of us started to get camera-shy. Truth be told we should have gone straight through them. But, believe it or not, although you are in the heat of the moment, you've got that little fellow in the back of your mind telling you, 'You're on *Big Brother*. Every move is being watched.'

Maybe that's why things were so much better on the Fulham Road in the hours leading up to kickoff. I didn't throw a punch after the game but before it me and other pals threw plenty of punches. As it happens my efforts to avoid detection turned out to be a waste of time. There were no less than five different cameras on me as I had gone about my unlawful business: two council closed-circuit-television cameras, one hand-held complete with police commentary, one above the shops and the fifth in an Old Bill helicopter. Everything I did would be there in high definition for the authorities to pore over at their leisure. Given what happened to me later I wouldn't have got any more bird anyway, even if I had got into a full-blown tear-up.

But all that was for another day. In the immediate aftermath we had mixed feelings. We were aware that the Soul Crew took liberties with other firms, which we didn't let happen. But with the arrests and the bird that was handed out I feel that I should have done more to justify my sentence.

They had come for an altercation. And we had obliged them.

1

Must Try Harder

I was born in Isleworth, West London in 1967. My mum, Rosemary, was from Tooting my dad, Graham, from Richmond. My parents went their separate ways when I was three and at first I went to live with my gran, my dad's mother, in East Sheen. Later, when Dad had remarried, he got a house in Whitton, west London and I moved in with him and his new wife.

I have heard all the bollocks about kids going off the rails when their parents split up. To me, that's what it is. Bollocks. I can honestly say it didn't affect me that much. People always bring divorce up when they are trying to explain how this one and that one went off the rails. They never say 'it was in his nature to be violent or to be a tea leaf' but, nine times out of ten, that is the truth. It certainly was for me.

I am not blaming my parents for anything. They were both honest grafters who gave me a good example to follow. Dad was a black-taxi driver, one of London's legendary cabbies, a man who had done the 'knowledge' and worked hard to make a living. Mum was a florist, and a bloody good one too, dedicated to running her shops.

My first school was Heathfield primary and my senior years were spent at Whitton secondary. I was a pain in the arse to the teachers, probably from day one if truth be told. They did their best for us but to me the whole thing was an excuse for a laugh and a joke. I often bunked off but even that was boring. You had to find something to do away from school and that wasn't always easy.

If my former classmates were describing me now I am sure they would say I was a real piss-taker, a joker, a comedian. It didn't matter who it was, or where I was, there was just no stopping me. One time, when I was fifteen, I was at the top of the stairs when I saw a hard-man teacher. My mate dared me to throw a ball at the top of his bald head.

'I bet you a quid you won't throw it at him,' he whispered, conspiratorially.

'Just watch me,' I thought.

Two seconds later the ball had bounced off his 'canister', sending him into a right fucking rage. We ran along the corridor at top speed into our classroom. He stormed in and called me out. Obviously, I had been grassed up, because it would have been impossible for him to have seen who had done it.

'You are going to the headmaster's office Marriner,' he fumed.

I was told to stand outside the office while Silly Bollocks went in to see the head, no doubt demanding that I be severely punished for assaulting a teacher. I was called into the office where the head told me I was going to be caned.

'You have a choice Marriner. You can either have three on one hand and three on the other, four on one hand and two on the other or all six on one hand.'

The man was all heart.

'Three on each,' I reluctantly told him, although there was no proof of my 'crime'.

I put my right hand out and he raised the cane to shoulder height, ready to whack me. But as he brought the bendy wooden implement down I pulled my hand away, making him miss the intended target. He was entitled to know why I had dodged his cane. After all he had been good enough to give me the choice of how many blows I could have on each hand.

I felt my explanation was reasonable enough.

'Go fuck yourself, you prick. My dad don't hit me so don't fucking think you are going to.'

His expression was a mixture of shock and anger. I had a good idea what was coming next.

'I have no alternative but to suspend you,' he sternly informed me.

'Yeah, fucking blinding,' I replied and with that I stormed out.

At the front door of the school I bumped into a prefect.

'You can't come this way,' he said.

'I can do what the fuck I like, you cunt. I have just been suspended. So get out the fucking way.'

Having faced the head, I knew there was now a higher power I would have to answer to: my father. Unless that is I could somehow intercept the dreaded letter from school saying what a naughty boy I had been. I got up early for the next few days and, sure enough, when the head's unwanted letter dropped on the mat I scooped it up and tore it to pieces. It didn't do me much good because someone grassed me up and told my old man. He was quite strict, or at least he tried to be, but I could always tell that he didn't really mean it. He wanted the best for me and probably put on an act to keep me in line. It rarely worked.

As well as taking the piss out of the teachers I also got into my fair share of fights. I hung around with other lads who were quite handy and one or other of us always seemed to be involved in a scrap. It was around this time that I had my collar felt for the first time. I heard that someone had given my brother a dig, something that just wasn't on. I bided my time, waiting for the right moment to avenge my brother. Later that day when council workers were mowing the school lawn I saw my chance. I picked up a spade and whacked the kid with it. The police were called and I got off with a caution. But that was me on the rocky road.

I eventually left school at the age of fifteen, but not before I managed to get myself expelled twice after being suspended on numerous occasions. I remember the first time as clearly as if it was yesterday. We were sitting out in the corridor when my pal Mark gave me a boiled sweet. As I sucked on the sweet I had my feet up on the chair in front of me. This was too much for the teacher.

'Take your feet off the chair and take that sweet out of your mouth,' he barked.

I didn't move an inch and crunched hard on the sweet, smiling sarcastically.

The teacher kicked the chair from under me.

'Get up Marriner.'

What was all this about, using surnames?

'My name's Jason,' I reminded him.

'There's not a teacher in this school who doesn't know who you are.'

'You can carry on talking to me like that you prick and you'll know who I am,' I replied.

He noticed that I was wearing a Fred Perry T-shirt and that my tie was halfway down my front.

'While we're at it you can do your tie up. You should also be wearing a school shirt.'

'I didn't realise this was a fashion parade.'

He leant over and put his hands on me, trying his best to do my tie up.

'Get your hands off me, you mongrel,' I said.

He carried on being heavy-handed. With that I nutted him, my forehead catching him on the nose. I felt cushty as I didn't like the cunt.

Two minutes later I was once again in front of the head.

'This is unacceptable and despicable behaviour. I have no option but to expel you.'

Even though I was being thrown out they didn't give up on me. The school, the educational board, a welfare officer and a social worker called a meeting. What do you do with a problem like Jason Marriner, they asked themselves? Send him to a psychiatrist, that's what. I thought the idea was a bit extreme, but they had to be seen to be doing something, not least because the teachers were expecting it. It was strange because my registration teacher, who I got on really well with, was married to the bloke I had head-butted.

So that is how, for the only time in my life, I ended up seeing a shrink. It wasn't how you imagine it from the movies: lying on a couch while a man with an East European accent hypnotises you, asks about your relationship with your parents and how many times a day you wank.

No, I was given simple English and arithmetic tests, which were followed by exercises so absurd that I still laugh about it today. At the end they handed me wooden shapes: squares that I had to slot into squares, circles into circles, triangles into triangles. I don't think they were taking the piss, but I wasn't about to give them the benefit of the doubt.

I stood up and threw the shapes across the room.

'Are you fucking joking? I'm fifteen, not fucking two.'

Weeks later, when the verdict came back from the psychiatrist, it was an even bigger joke. 'Jason has a short fuse . . .' the report read. Well, fuck me, what a revelation! I really needed a shrink to tell me that.

I never went back to school after that. It was the best solution for everyone, especially my teachers.

2

The Drug Kicks in

It wasn't inevitable that I would become a Chelsea fan. I was born in west London, in Isleworth. The overwhelming majority of kids at our school certainly weren't of a blue persuasion, even if it was in what you might call a Chelsea area. In fact there were just as many Man U, Liverpool and Arsenal as there were Chelsea.

It all came down to Dad, as it probably does for most sons. He was Chelsea through and through and that was good enough for me. I started going to Stamford Bridge with him at the age of five. My first game was an evening kickoff but as I was so young I didn't have a clue who we were playing. I remember the atmosphere: the pungent smell of hamburgers; the programme sellers calling out to the passing fans; the huge queues of men with blue scarves waiting impatiently to get into the Shed. Being a kid some of the sights and sounds mystified me. I couldn't work out why the police were taking laces out of people's Doc Marten boots or why some fans had blue-and-white silk scarves wrapped around their wrists.

One thing I did know. I was hooked.

Football was now my life. I loved it long before I got into hooliganism. And I still do. I can watch tennis, a bit of athletics, rugby internationals (although only if England are involved). But give me the beautiful game and I am all over it like a cheap suit.

I never let work interfere with football. My first job, when I was still at school, was a milk round. But I always got away early for games. The milkman's brother was a massive Chelsea fan and he understood why I needed to make myself scarce on Saturdays. It was the same when I started doing day release from school as a carpet fitter. The company I worked for, Hollygrove, wasn't quite as understanding as the milkman. Things came to a head when we were due to play Man United away on a Wednesday night. In the run up to the match I had been having great banter with one of the other carpet fitters – a Cockney Red called Steve Jones – and I was desperate to go. It meant taking a day off but I was told that if I missed work I would be sacked. I loved the job and the people I worked with so it should have been a real dilemma. But it wasn't. It was no contest. I went up to Manchester. Lucky for me my job was still there on the Thursday morning.

I have always been a grafter and a good earner and that didn't change when I went to football. In those days a good pal of mine ran a coach – which later got a great reputation – from the Red Lion in Twickenham. There would be four or five of us who had an input on the coach, with all of us taking bookings. Nine times out of ten it would be the same fifty-four people on the coach although sometimes we got a double-decker, which could take about seventy-five.

I would take fifteen of my mates along and charge them £10 each for the bus fare, passing on £8 a head to the driver. That meant I had £30 in my pocket. At the time Dad was a publican so I would take two cases of his lager onto the coach. I knocked out the ale to the boys on the bus, which was gone before we got to the end of the street. After I had paid the old man for the beer, which I got at face value, I had £15 left. That was £45 profit, good money for a kid earning about fifteen quid a day as a carpet fitter.

Some of my money-making schemes weren't so six-and-eight. In those days there were no alarm systems on cigarette machines and fruit machines, and every pub we visited had at least one of each. Always aware of good earning opportunities I would go well prepared. I robbed the fag machines with a screwdriver and sold what I got out of them to the other lads. I then moved onto the fruit machines, which I played with a coin attached to a wire, scooping up jackpot after jackpot. I used beer mats from Dad's pub and towels to deafen the sound of coins tinkling into the metal receptacle. It also helped that there were two hundred or so Chelsea boys drinking and joking in the bar. The noise they made was deafening.

It wouldn't be long before I took my first steps into the world of football violence. I had witnessed it from the age of eight but didn't really understand what they were fighting about. Then as I became an adolescent the arguments would start with other boys about the teams we supported. 'Chelsea are shit,' they would say. The rage inside me was indescribable – even if I now have to admit Chelsea *were* shit – and quite often it came to blows. I had had my first fight about football and there was no turning back.

The first incident at a game was away to Wolves, on 22 January 1983, when I was fifteen. I was standing with my pal Darren Crewe on a grass verge outside their ground when he asked me to hold a Union Jack with 'Chelsea' written on it. It maybe wasn't the best place to be holding a flag like that given there were mobs of Wolves on the prowl. Within seconds one of them was on my case.

'Does that say Chelsea on there, mate?' he growled.

'Yeah,' I replied.

'Fuck off then.'

He had a mate with him, a big black geezer. So it was two grown men against a kid. They came at me. The black bloke took a swing at my head but missed. I spat at him and at the same time tried to catch him with a right hook. When I also failed to connect he chased me round the car park and when he caught up with me and I ended up with a shiny black eye and a kicking.

Word of what happened spread through the Chelsea ranks like wildfire and it appeared that I wasn't the only one to have got a clump. Wolves had been taking liberties with a few people, something that our lot couldn't let go. They went looking for revenge after the game and gave those responsible a right going over. I knew it wasn't just me who had been attacked but that didn't matter. The same thoughts kept swirling around in my head, over and over again.

'This is my family. They are doing it for me. They knew I came unstuck. They weren't having it. They are fighting for me.'

My gratitude was overwhelming. From that day on I was Chelsea.

3

Roker Park, Via the Bluebell

By the time I was sixteen or seventeen, in the early-to-mid Eighties, I was beginning to get right into the scene, which had changed out of all recognition since the Seventies. That was a time when huge groups of fans steamed in to each other on the terraces, the main objective being to take the other lot's end. There was little or no organisation involved; we charged and they charged back in huge waves, with the Old Bill doing their best to keep the two sides apart.

By the time I became a player, football violence was getting better and better organised and we either had to keep up or face the prospect of taking a beating every week. Lucky for us Hickey was a brilliant planner and strategist and with him at the helm we often got the better of the other mob just because of the way he went about things. The best example was on 13 February 1984 when we went up to Mackem-land to play Sunderland in the semi-final of the Milk Cup.

The club had been given a big allocation of tickets and it was expected that about ten thousand Chelsea would be travelling from London for the game, which was on a Wednesday night. I went up on a double-decker coach from Twickenham along with the best part of eighty other very game lads, all well up for it, while Hickey was on another coach, which was also full of known faces. Meanwhile many others in the firm made their own arrangements. There would be fucking hundreds of us there.

The long trek to the north-east started early in the morning. It was a long and very boring journey, which was made a little more bearable by us making right fucking nuisances of ourselves when we stopped at the motorway service stations. To keep ourselves going on the bus we got stuck into cans of lager – there was little or no cocaine about in those days – and after seven hours of solid drinking some of us were legless by the time we got to Gateshead, where we had arranged to meet Hickey's coach.

One lad was really pissed. His nickname was Oddball and he had tagged along with Stuart Glass, one of our best-known faces. Hickey was not a happy camper. One minute I was standing chatting to him about the plan of action and the next he was doing his nut.

'Who is that man? Who is that?' he said in that posh voice of his.

'Oh he's all right, Steve. He's with us. That's Oddball,' I replied, with a smile on my face.

I failed miserably. To Steve 'Hickey' Hickmott, football hooliganism was a serious business. He wouldn't tolerate anyone who might let Chelsea down.

'All right? All right?' he fumed. 'He's not all right. He's paralytic drunk. Get him on the coach.'

Oddball didn't take offence at Hickey. He couldn't. He didn't have a clue what day it was. In fact, he fell over and hit his head on the kerb.

'Get that man on the coach. We have come here for a war.'

It was funny the way Hickey said it in those precise and clipped tones, almost like an army officer screaming orders to his men. But I knew he was deadly serious. We *had* come for a war, one he had been planning for weeks. He calculated that if we met up at Gateshead and used public transport for the last part of our journey it would throw the Old Bill off the scent.

So Oddball was bundled onto the coach and we continued on our journey, still drinking and talking excitedly about what was to come. When the buses parked up we hopped on the metro for the short journey to decrepit old Roker Park, which was Sunderland's ground in those days. We got off at Seaburn station and what a mob it was. There must have been five hundred of us, all itching to get at the Mackems.

Now all we had to do was find the cunts.

That turned out to be easier than we thought. We turned left, in the direction of the stadium. There was a pub diagonally across from us called the Blue Bells. It was their main boozer and it was full of them. Bingo!

We did not hesitate. We charged straight at the pub, giving them no time at all. They were taken completely by surprise, as were the Old Bill, who were nowhere to be seen. The pub got smashed to pieces with every window put through and their lads inside getting a real kicking, while our boys also managed to pick off groups of Sunderland on the outside. Chelsea were just too powerful for them on the night. What a fucking result and all thanks to Hickey's master plan.

There were major battles inside the stadium with the cozzers, and then, after the game, it was very hairy. Large, angry mobs of Sunderland were prowling the streets looking for revenge for the Blue Bells. The Old Bill didn't help our cause. First they split us up and then they wouldn't let us go the way we wanted. Half of us ended up mixed in with Sunderland, but the cozzers didn't give a fuck. It was either their way or get nicked.

Back in London, a few days after the game, I was talking to a pal, Tony Rolph, who didn't make it back to our coach.

'Did you get nicked, Tony?' I asked.

'No, I couldn't find my way back to the coach. The Old Bill made me walk to the station over the bridge with all the fucking Sunderland fans. I kept my head down and my mouth shut because I was shitting myself.'

Apart from the post-match chaos (and the result, we lost 2–0) it had been a great night. Hickey had done us proud as he would do so many times.

And he was right about Oddball being a liability. On the way back he woke up, turned round to Stuart Glass and said: 'We must be there soon.' The silly cunt was so drunk that he thought we were still on our way up to Wearside. We had had untold pitched battles, lost two-nil, he had taken a head knock, plus we were halfway home. Yet he still asked if we were there yet!

As Hickey had pointed out, he really was of no fucking use to us.

4

A Smashing Time at Parsons Green

The second leg against Sunderland was only six days later. The Old Bill were expecting trouble and they were right to. We knew the Mackems would come down in their thousands with a good strong squad: after all we had smashed up their boozer and had untold rows at their ground. So they would have the hump for sure. As their coaches arrived there were lots of scallywags bricking the windows, with mobs of Chelsea waiting for Sunderland to do to us what we had done to them. Unfortunately, the cozzers were right on the ball and quickly defused the situation.

Our mood wasn't helped by events on the pitch. We went down 3–2, which gave them an aggregate victory of 5–2, a result that pissed us right off, especially as a former Chelsea hero, Clive 'Flasher' Walker, was playing for Sunderland. A good mate of mine lost the plot, ran onto the pitch and attacked Walker. But that was about it as far as the Mackems were concerned. The Old Bill were out in huge numbers and spoiled our party.

It was time for Plan B. It was time to get our own back on the ICF.

Rewind six months, to 15 September 1983. Chelsea were playing West Ham, at home, in a league match. Unusually for away teams they brought their full mob to the Bridge and even more unusually they took the piss. I can laugh about it now but at the time I didn't see the funny side.

I am a good friend of ICF main man Carlton Leach these days. But, back in the day, when we were probably the two top mobs in the country, Chelsea and West Ham were bitter rivals. And they were good; they were very, very good. Well-organised, with a hardcore of some of the most formidable thugs in England, the ICF had to be treated with respect at all times. Put it this way, they didn't lose many.

As with many offs, it was the element of surprise that did for us that day. I was in the west stand and I could clearly hear the Shed taunting West Ham.

'Where's your famous ICF?' they chanted, pointing as one to the away end, where they thought West Ham's mob were.

All of a sudden a huge roar went up from the Shed. It wasn't the Headhunters, it was the ICF. They had somehow got into our sacred place and now they intended to take even more liberties. The fighting started at the back of the Shed and cascaded down to the bottom of the terracing and then onto the pitch. Some of our blokes hate to admit it but the ICF definitely got the better of it. It was round one to them.

West Ham weren't finished yet. The ICF were also in the west stand and I saw a big group walking across the seats to get at us. There were very few of our lads around as it was so early. I thought, 'Fuck me. It's on top here. We are going to get eaten alive.' We did our best, me and the few other Headhunters who were already in the ground. I managed to throw a lot of punches but I was probably taking even more in return, including many dull ones to the head. We might well have been battered if the cavalry hadn't arrived. Seeing what was going on, more and more of our lot were piling in and we were now giving as good as we got. Let's call it honours even for that one.

Although we salvaged a bit of honour in the west stand it couldn't disguise the fact that we came unstuck. And in our own backyard. They had come into our end, started a ruck and driven us onto the pitch. For a mob of our calibre that was unacceptable. There was a bitter taste in our mouths and we swore that a day of judgement would soon follow.

It resulted in an unbelievable night of football violence.

Fast forward to the aftermath of the second leg with Sunderland. We couldn't get at the Mackems because the Old Bill had it boxed off, but there might be an alternative, one that would give us even more satisfaction. West Ham were at Wimbledon that night and we knew they would have to stop at Parsons Green tube on the way home. So some of us sneaked away from Stamford Bridge, still under siege by the Old Bill, and went to look for the ICF. It was a real mob of front-runners too, blokes who would not hesitate to use extreme violence. As the saying goes, 'all the right faces were in the right places'.

We waited patiently for the train to arrive and sure enough, minutes later, it pulled in. The carriages were jam-packed with West Ham, both ordinary fans and mob. They didn't have a care in the world but little did they know the platform was full of Chelsea. The doors slid open and we started chanting, 'Ooh, ooh, ooh.'

We took them completely by surprise. I could see the fear in their eyes.

We steamed the train, punching and kicking every cunt within range. It was total mayhem. They were petrified, screaming and shouting. I am sure there were ordinary fans on the train but it's only the same as they did to our scarfers at our place. We wanted to send out a message not just to West Ham but to all mobs: 'Let this be a lesson to you. Don't come to Stamford Bridge and take fucking liberties.'

It wasn't just fists and feet. My memory is of one of our boys pulling a fire extinguisher off the station wall and smashing it through the train window, spraying the passengers inside the carriage with a thousand glass fragments. Still not satisfied he threw the extinguisher at one of the West Ham lads, hitting him full force on the head. Other lads had bricks and were hurling them at the windows. And all the while we sang, 'Where's your famous ICF?' It went berserk and there were hardly any windows left on the train.

That wasn't enough for us. The next time we were at Upton Park was in April 1985. Throughout the game we were singing 'Victoria, Victoria', our way of inviting them to meet us after the game. They were up for it and I remember hundreds of us getting off the train at Victoria, walking past New Scotland Yard and ending up at Shakes wine bar. There were masses of Japanese tourists around and they must have wondered why the fuck three hundred smartly dressed young men were marching through central London with grimly determined looks on their faces.

West Ham won't admit it but we chased them out of Shakes, then along the road and finally down the stairs of Victoria tube station, all the while chanting, 'Where's your famous ICF?' Everyone has seen it.

I am afraid the truth is we all get run, or done, sometime.

5

The Young Tearaway

I didn't just turn to violence at football. There were six other days in the week and my view was: why waste them? As a teenager I had lots of mates, mates that I would be out drinking and having a good time with. I am not saying it went off every night but, once we were lagging, trouble was just round the corner. It was like putting salt and vinegar on your fish and chips, a normal part of my life.

When I was about seventeen I lived in Hanworth and we used to do a lot of our socialising in Twickenham. I remember this Friday night me and my pals were in a pub called the King's Head. At chucking-out time there was no club nearby that we could go on to, but we wanted to carry on drinking. Walking down Twickenham high street we passed a fish-and-chip shop, which was closed, but there was loud music coming from the flat above. Somebody had organised a party.

You know what it's like at that age. When you are full of drink, and in high spirits, the last thing you want to do is go home. One of the lads decided to knock on the door and when it was answered we tried to blag our way in, even though we didn't have any drink with us. The people in the flat told us in no uncertain terms that we weren't coming in, which led to a bit of a commotion. That, in turn, led to more people in the party coming to the front door to see what the fuck was going on.

There were only three or four of us: me, Paul Winter, Carl Stenhouse and Kieran Whelan, three Yids I might add, all of them being Spurs fans. We were quickly getting outnumbered. As one of the tenants of the flat made it very clear that we had no chance of getting in a little scuffle broke out. It didn't take long to escalate. I spotted a milk crate and so I grabbed a couple of the empty bottles and chucked them at the people in the doorway.

The best was yet to come.

I don't know what made me do it but I picked up the crate, and, bang! I threw it at the chip shop's big plate-glass window, smashing it into little pieces. The shop alarm immediately went off so that was us, in the middle of a high street which was pretty busy, even at that time of night, with a noise that would have woken the dead blaring out. Our chances of avoiding detection were somewhere between extremely slim and non-existent.

I did my best to get away, but it was short-lived. The Old Bill arrested us and although I pretended to have no knowledge of the incident I was held in the cells overnight. On the Saturday our foes from the flat came to the station to give statements about what we had done, which resulted in me being charged with criminal damage. We were eventually released, on the Sunday evening, but I later ended up down the Richmond magistrates court, where I got a fine. That was it in those days: a slap on the wrist and a fine, at least for some offences.

My next brush with the law was a bit more serious. In fact it could have seen me going down for a long time. It was a typical Friday night. I had been in the George in Twickenham and left the pub about eleven to go back to my nan's in East Sheen. She had a spare room and I often used it as a bolthole. In fact the reason I was going to Nan's was because I wanted to catch an early-morning train and her house was near the station. Chelsea were playing up north and from there I would go into London to get a train from a mainline station.

There was a bus stop right outside the George and from there I could get a bus right to the top of Nan's road. My mates had already left and gone their separate ways and so I was standing at the bus stop on my own. For whatever reason a fella came towards me and said, 'Move away from the bus stop.'

I had never seen this herbert before, or his pal. I didn't have a clue who he was. I told them I was waiting for a bus to take me home.

One of them pulled out a warrant card.

'If you don't move you'll get nicked.'

They was half at the bully game and they shuffled me down the street for about ten yards. Out of the corner of my eye I see a couple of my pals. I decided to turn right and to make my way down George Street.

The two Old Bill, both obviously plain-clothes, had a question for me.

'Where do you think you are going now?'

'Fuck me. I can't win. What I'd actually like to do is get a bus. But you won't let me do that.'

One of them put his hands on me and tried to pin me up against the wall. 'No more,' I said.

I nutted the cunt straight on his nose.

They steamed into me. I tried to kick and punch my way out of it but they were getting the better of me and I was getting done.

Lucky for me the mates I had just seen came running across and they steamed into the Old Bill. We ended up kicking fuck out of them. Another pal, who happened to be driving that night, pulled up in a side street. I jumped into his car and off we sped, more than happy that the tables had been turned.

Violence over for the night? You must be fucking joking.

As we were driving I spotted a close friend of mine, Jakesy. He was arguing with some fellas outside McDonald's. I jumped out of the car and asked him:

'What's up Jakesy?'

'Nothing Jase. Just these leery cunts.'

We were outnumbered by the leery cunts but I was in good company as Jakesy has always been one game kid. I whacked one of the geezers and as scuffles broke out other pals joined in. We were known as a game little herd in the pubs and on the streets: me, Jakesy, Rocky and Matty and as usual we did ourselves proud in the row.

Next thing I knew I was across the bonnet of a car, fighting this one fella when, all of a sudden, I heard an almighty scream. As I turned round I saw Jakesy's eyes almost popping out of his head. He had hold of a geezer's bollocks and he was squeezing them as hard as he could.

Then after just a few minutes we heard them: the wail of Old Bill sirens. Little did Jakesy know that not two minutes ago me and some of our other pals had been kicking fuck out of two cozzers. I had it on my Bromleys but the Old Bill stopped me and handcuffed me to railings as they arrested some of my pals. So there I was, attached to these railings as every cunt and his dog walked past. Eventually, they put me in the back of a meat wagon.

We were driven to Twickenham police station, which is about five hundred yards down the road. I said to Jakesy: 'I'm bang in egg and bacon here.'

In the station, lucky for me, they've got a full house. So they take us to a holding station in Teddington, a few miles away. All I've got on my mind is the two cozzers we had ironed out. If I'm being honest I was over the moon to be in Teddington nick because from what I was told the two Old Bill had sustained quite a few injuries. As you can imagine they take that sort of thing very seriously and they were out scouring the streets looking for the people who had done their mates. Little did they know I was in one of their cells, which is the only time I have ever been happy to be behind the door.

I eventually get charged with ABH for the fight outside McDonald's and released. If it ever had come on top for the fight with the cozzers my defence would have been I couldn't have been in two places at once. Jakesy and Co later found out about the two Old Bill and said I was mad for doing what I did. But we are still close friends to this day.

As for the cozzers who accosted me at the bus stop I will never find out why they picked on me. Probably because they thought they could bully and intimidate people and get away with it. But they came unstuck that night. To some what I did by nutting an Old Bill might seem extreme but I couldn't have given a fuck. When you are young, you have no fear, nothing to lose.

Actually, the most outrageous thing was that they made me miss a Chelsea away game.

* * *

Growing up in the Eighties I had many lads' holidays in the likes of Spain and one I remember well was in Fuengirola. I was there with my close pal, Lee Scott, and a few others. One night we bumped into some other good pals from home, the likes of Jakesy, Robert Honeyball, Matty Morris and Winston Connery. Being Londoners we used to go to a gaff called the London Pub, and after a few beers we more often than not ended up in a nightclub next door, the London Underground.

That's where it kicked off.

To this day I am not sure how it started but I saw Matty with his hands round a bloke's throat. They had obviously had some kind of altercation. The bouncers came and broke it up but, Matty being Matty, he couldn't leave it. Next thing you know the doormen are dragging him up the stairs and out onto the street.

Us being the young game tearaways we were, we ended up fighting the doormen. To be fair we were holding our own and doing quite well. Until that is they started shouting in Spanish for back up. They were in luck. We were fighting next to a taxi rank. So the drivers – who had been standing around, smoking and waiting for a fare, as cabbies do – decided to weigh into us as well. Obviously, this meant that we were greatly outnumbered. But before it went much further we heard the wail of police sirens in the distance. When the Old Bill turned up, they got out of their cars and started talking away to us in Spanish. That wasn't one of the subjects I did at school, so I had no fucking idea what they were saying.

But after the spic doormen and cabbies had finished grassing us up I didn't need to be fluent in Spanish to work out what they and the Old Bill had been on about. That's because we got cuffed and thrown into the back of the police motors. After that we got taken to the police station, where we were held until the next day.

After discussing the situation with the Spanish duty solicitor, and being told we were being taken straight to court, the simplest and easiest option was to hold our hands up and plead guilty. So I did, fully expecting that I was going to get a spell in a Spanish nick. But I was more than happy when, instead, we all got fined. I can't remember how much it was, but I do remember smiling at Jakesy. We were in the dock and I tapped the wooden edge. It meant, 'You're knocked.' In other words, we weren't going to pay.

Make up your own mind if we paid the fine . . . or bought a few more rounds of San Miguel.

* * *

I worked for a firm called Tower Demolition in East Sheen, whose yard was next door to a pub, the Belvedere, owned by an ex-Fulham player, Les Strong. Every Friday we would be straight in there after work and this night was no different. We were all drinking, my work pals and I, and there was a discussion about going home and getting changed and going on to another pub, Canes, which was not that far from the Belvedere.

For me to go home, get changed and come back was a mission but I could go to Nan's, to my little bolthole, where I had spare clothes and a room for later if I wanted it. So after a few hours in the Belvedere we went our separate ways and arranged to meet in Canes, which was very lively and popular, the 'in' place.

I went to my dear old Nan's to get changed and before I left she said, 'Be good and stay out of trouble.'

And as I gave her a kiss goodbye I replied, as I always did, 'Of course, Nan.'

I got into Canes, where my workmates had been joined by many other pals. Everyone was in good spirits. The drinks were flowing and as the night got older we were getting drunker and drunker. Then as so often happened a littler argument started with a group of lads from outside the area, from Putney, lads who had been drawn to Canes thanks to its reputation as *the* place to go.

I can't remember how or who started it but it kicked right off between us and them. One of their lads got a bad head injury when his head was whacked off the rail around the bar. With the level of violence in Canes we knew the Old Bill would be keen to track down those who had been involved.

And that's how it turned out. Over the next few days ten lads were arrested – among them Ziggy, Scott McGill, Sean Baker, Jason Solomon, Buzby, Gary Bolton and Les Winslade – with six being charged. The rumour was that the cozzers were looking for a seventh man but had no idea who he was. As usual they put pressure on the lads who had been nicked to give them a name.

When they were giving their statements the lads mentioned the name Jason. Unfortunately, at this point, one of our group dropped me right in it. I won't identify him because he was young and naive and I know he didn't mean to do it. But when 'Jason' was mentioned he turned round to the Old Bill and said: 'That's Jason Marriner, not black Jason [our pal Jason Solomon is black].'

The cozzers were over the moon. They thought they had rung the bell and turned up the missing piece in the jigsaw. It took a while for them to track me down but eventually they did. I was taken to Richmond police station, where I was charged with ABH and affray. After a silent interview (I have made it a rule to keep silent, not even giving them a 'no comment') and a night in the cells I appeared before Richmond magistrates court. The Old Bill tried to get me remanded but I was given bail, with one of the conditions being that I was not allowed to enter the Canes public house. I was also put on a curfew: I could not leave the house from seven in the evening until seven in the morning.

These conditions were in force until my trial, which was ten months later in Isleworth Crown Court. Five of the accused pleaded guilty at the earliest possible opportunity and would be sentenced at a later date. So, as the jury was sworn in, that left me, Jason Solomon and Scott McGill. Then Jason Solomon's barrister submitted that his client had 'no case to answer'. The judge agreed and instructed the jury to find Jason not guilty, which it did. Scott had a separate charge to me of carrying an offensive weapon and had, like me, had been charged with affray but not with ABH.

Scott took the decision to go into the box and give evidence. I don't remember much about it but I do clearly remember him being torn apart by the prosecution. And to my dying day I will never forget the following exchange:

'You had a knife on you Scott, didn't you?' the prosecuting barrister asked.

'I did,' Scott replied.

'What kind of knife was it?'

'A butterfly knife.'

'What were you going to do with that knife?'

'I was just going to give him a quick cut.'

That was the moment I decided I wouldn't be taking the stand. I couldn't help but laugh because, even at the age of twenty, I thought, 'Why would you admit that in front of a jury?' There was another reason for not taking the stand: I had worked out that they didn't have much on me, so why let them twist things and make the jury think otherwise.

The trial lasted for a few days and eventually the verdicts came back.

'Do you find the defendant Jason Marriner guilty or not guilty on count one of actual bodily harm?'

'Not guilty.'

'Do you find Jason Marriner guilty or not guilty on count two of affray?'

'Not guilty.'

I gave my own verdict.

'Get in there,' I said.

Trust me. Getting a not guilty is a wicked feeling.

The same process is gone through for Scott and he gets a guilty on the offensive-weapon charge. Because of his open admission he gets twelve months in the warehouse.

I caught a bus to the White Hart in Whitton and on the way I meet Kath Scott, the mum of my lifelong, and closest, friend Lee Scott. Kath was like a mum to me as well. I tell her my result and she gives me a kiss and a cuddle. Because the bus was packed there were people standing and as I was cuddling Kath I was trying to work out where I had seen this other female passenger. It suddenly dawned on me. She had been on the jury. She smiled at me and I smiled back.

'Thank you,' I said.

She didn't say a word but her smile said it all.

I went on the piss that night and two days later I organised my trip to West Germany for the 1988 European Championships. Little did I know that in the years to come I would have a return fixture at Isleworth Crown Court.

6

Meet the Headhunters

Before I go any further I want you to meet some of my best mates. Boys who have backed up in the tightest spots, boys who have rucked toe-to-toe alongside me. Like me, they are genuine blokes who love their football and their fighting.

Steve 'Hickey' Hickmott

You met him in the Mackems chapter but he deserves to be first in this one. In the Eighties he was definitely the captain of the team, our main man. We work mainly as a unit these days but that doesn't mean there was anything wrong with having a leader – at least not when he is like Hickey. I looked up to him in my younger days and despite that posh Tunbridge Wells accent he was always at the front when a row kicked off and he always got stuck in.

He organised and orchestrated everything – so I can blame the cunt for me doing so much bird for Chelsea! Only joking. And that was another thing about him – he has a fantastic sense of humour and we have great banter to this day. We really needed to get ourselves organised because other mobs, especially the ICF, were moving in that direction. Organisation was often the difference between running a mob and taking a beating.

Hickey got done for FV as part of Operation Own Goal but he later turned the tables on the Old Bill by getting the case thrown out on appeal. Even better he took the filth for a hundred grand compensation after they were found to have fitted him up. He now lives in the Far East and I don't mean Leytonstone! The proper Far East with jungles, rice paddies and mobile-phone factories. He rarely makes it home to England but whenever he does we always get together. Hickey will never lose his sense of humour, although he will never be as funny as me and he knows it!

One time on a visit back home he met me at Chelsea. As it was the day of a game the Old Bill were watching the pub we were meeting in. All of a sudden this limo pulls up outside. Out steps Hickey. He hadn't changed a bit; in fact he was still wearing his old Doc Martens, his combat jacket and the jeans he had been wearing for the last 344 years. Spotting the coppers he went into a typical Hickey routine, eloquent as fuck.

'Hello Inspector. I'm just quaffing champagne the government bought for me. Operation Own Goal? What an own goal that was. Fabricated evidence. Tut, tut, tut. Anyway, cheers old boy.'

The Old Bill didn't see the funny side – those cunts have no sense of humour – but we were pissing ourselves.

It doesn't matter that he is thousands of miles from home; Hickey is still Chelsea, England and a football hooligan and always will be. Just look at his daily routine. Every morning, without fail, he gets up, polishes his Doc Martens and as the sun is rising he runs the St George's Cross up the flagpole and salutes it.

I am sure he thanks the British government for giving him a right few quid – and let me tell you the cunt's still got it. He's that tight he wakes up in the middle of the night to make sure he ain't lost no sleep.

Steve, my friend, I salute you.

Andrew 'Nightmare' Frain

I got to know Andy, who is from Reading, through meeting him week in, week out at Chelsea. He was just always on the scene. We hit it off straight away and became close friends, going drinking together outside of football. There is no doubt that he is one of the most notorious football hooligans in Britain

In the crazy world of football violence you get all different kinds of people: nutters; out-and-out lunatics; jokers; educated types; ordinary blokes in dead-end occupations; characters with big personalities and life's introverts.

Andy is a nutter, pure and simple. But he is a nice nutter. A football mob might have five or six hundred blokes but it's always the same thirty or forty at the front. I was always at the front but I am not a nutter; I was at the front because that is where you are meant to be, because I was part of a firm, because I wanted to back up my mates and to have a row. Andy by contrast was always at the front because he always wanted to get stuck in.

His nickname is Nightmare and he is very good at living up to that name.

Ian and Dave Sim

They are identical twins and are known to all and sundry as – you've guessed it – 'the twins'. They hail from Kent and I have known them for many, many years, both in and out of the football scene. I class both Ian and Dave as good friends. The twins are top blokes, happily married family men, but at the same time they are off-key, away with it! They are the gamest lads I have ever met, probably too game at times.

I can clearly remember Dave and me getting nicked together. It was late summer 1991, the day of the Charity Shield between Leeds and Liverpool. A massive Chelsea firm had been at a Madness concert in Finsbury Park and afterwards we went to the Holloway Tavern. The drink had been flowing all day: before the concert, during it in the beer tent and finally in the pub. It was now quite late at night and we were all lagging.

We weren't going home, at least not before we looked for Leeds or Liverpool, so we decided to go to King's Cross and see if they were about. On the way we ran into a group of about forty Derby lads on a stag do and had a small set-to with them, with a few punches being thrown. Then we got the message that there was a mob of Leeds Service Crew roaming about. That electrified us. They have a big reputation and there has been a fierce rivalry between the two clubs going back to the famous FA Cup final of 1970.

Just down the road from King's Cross we saw them. It was obvious from the way they were dressed that they were Service Crew. There was no eyeballing, no circling the wagons. We steamed in, letting them know in no uncertain terms we were Chelsea. More and more of our lads came round the corner and we were all getting stuck in: Dave, Ian and Nightmare among them. We ended up running Leeds.

Obviously, King's Cross is a busy, bustling, well-policed, camera-d-up area and within minutes Dave and I got arrested; first him, then me. We were sitting in the back of a police van having a right laugh about the whole thing when the Old Bill opened the doors and tried to squeeze another lad inside. The problem for them was that the newcomer was punching and kicking them and complaining bitterly about the way he was being treated.

'This is completely outrageous,' he said.

The newcomer was Andy Frain.

Dave and I were pissing ourselves about his attitude.

'Believe it or not Andy, if you do something illegal there is a chance you'll get nicked,' I told him.

It didn't do any good. He continued to berate the Old Bill for taking the liberty of arresting him. The next day Nightmare and I got released without charge but Dave got done for possession of a can of CS gas and got a fine and community service.

Martin King

Martin has written several books on the scene including *Hoolifan*. But he is a game lad, always to the fore in a ruck. He is a good pal in and out of football and I still speak to him once a week. I know his current girlfriend and his son and daughter and like many Chelsea he is a nice, honest, hard-working bloke – and, most importantly, a loyal friend.

When I was inside he visited me and wrote to me, as did Hickey and the twins and many others in the mob. Thanks lads, I will never forget your loyalty.

Mark Alleway

He was a very game kid, always in the front when it was on top, always in the thick of it. His brother Gary was also on the scene, although neither of them is involved now. Mark was charged for the off at the Three Guineas pub with West Ham, along with the twins, Nightmare and Tony Covelle and all five of them got remanded. This incident was where Barry Lewis, a West Ham fan, got a horrific slash across the face, which resulted in him needing sixty-seven stitches.

On the day of the trial the police turned up at Lewis's door to take him to court but, for whatever reason, no evidence against our lads was forthcoming and they all walked free. It was a massive relief for them as they were looking at very long jail sentences in the event of a guilty verdict.

I have been in a few hairy situations with the brothers Alleway, none more memorable than in a West End pub called the Chandos. A gang of us had been out on an all-day drinking session in Swiss Cottage: Fat Pat, Tony Murphy, Wayne Morley, Disco, Maggie, Swiggy, Andy Garner and quite a few others. A decision was then made: seven or eight of us went down to Leicester Square to carry on with our session. The pub we ended up in was a funny shape, with all sorts of nooks and crannies. We saw lads who were clearly from other firms although we didn't know which ones. All of a sudden I sensed tension in the air. Something was going to kick off.

My sixth sense was spot-on. I don't know how it started but someone ran up to our table and tried to bottle me. Luckily, as he drew his arm back ready to strike, Gary head-butted him full in the face. Gary may have saved my bacon but his quick thinking didn't do him any favours. A split second after he butted the geezer, Gary was glassed by someone sneaking up from the side. I fucking chinned the sly cunt, at which point the pub exploded.

The bottle and glasses were flying through the air and doing some serious damage to those who couldn't get out of the way in time. I picked up a bar stool, swinging it round my head and battering anything that moved. This went on for two or three minutes although, as is always the case, it seemed like much longer. The pub regulars and tourists were shocked and they cowered below tables, waiting for the violence to stop. The fighting went on outside and any bystander who was into that sort of thing would have really enjoyed it. It was a great off, made better because it was so unexpected.

It was only later that we discovered who our opponents were: Stoke's Naughty Forty crew, which didn't surprise us. They were always up for it.

Mark's time with the firm didn't last for much longer. A few years later we had organised a meet with another firm but for some reason very few of us turned up. Mark was disappointed and like the rest of us decided to call it a day and go home. On the tube he found a leaflet about a church and it started him thinking. His mother was a keen churchgoer and from that day on Mark was as well. My belief is that he substituted religion for the sheer adrenalin surge that football violence gave him. Thanks to his obsessive personality he gave the Headhunters 100 per cent and now he is giving God the same commitment. To me it was one addiction replacing another. I have never asked him which religion he follows – but I hope it is the Church of England!

Just because he goes to church instead of football doesn't make him less of a friend. God bless you Mark.

Billy Matthews

Billy is from Wandsworth and was once dubbed the 'Fat Man' by the media. In fact even Maggie Thatcher once said, 'We must catch the fat man.' Maggie's remarks followed a very high-profile incident down the King's Road in which Billy got found not guilty of a GBH section 18, but got four years for affray.

But I can assure you Billy is no longer fat. He is one of the staunchest and most loyal blokes you could ever meet and down-to-earth with it. The sort of bloke you would want beside you in a tight corner, or, if you were doing a bit behind the door, the sort you would want to do it with, simply because it would make the time go faster. I trust him with my life and he is a very good friend to this day and a top man.

Tony Covelle

I met Tony, who is from Kent, in the early Eighties and so he has been a good friend for thirty years or more. He is a front-runner, a game lad, who is well-respected not only by the Chelsea mob but also by mobs up and down the country. That respect is well-merited.

Tony also has a good sense of humour but he needs it as the years have started to catch up with him. Nowadays he pretends he is younger than he really is and he has claimed to be forty-five for the last eight years. You only have to look at him to see that he must have had an uphill paper round.

I have the utmost respect for Tony. Enough said!

Chris 'Chubby' Henderson

He was also a very good friend of mine who, sadly, has just passed away. He was partners with Hickey in the first ever football bar in Thailand, called the Dog's Bollocks, which became famous among football fans from all over the world. I met many good lads from other clubs in that bar.

Chubby got acquitted for Operation Own Goal and got £25,000 in compensation, which he used to open the bar. He was a funny character who knew how to tell a story and he will be sadly missed. RIP Chubby.

Kenny Goodwin

He is funny, a great character, good company and off his fucking head.

Kev Sweeney

Like many others an unsung hero and heavily involved back in the day. The biggest fight he has nowadays is trying to get him to wear a pair of jeans as he is stuck in the Eighties and still wears Farahs.

Jointy

Sadly, he is no longer with us. This man deserved the utmost respect. He was proper old school.

Skitzey

The clue is in the name. A proper gentleman – and a very good friend.

* * *

If I had had the space I could have mentioned dozens, maybe hundreds, of lads in this chapter. A number of them have been left out for very good reasons: some are still active while others have moved on. To all those I have missed it was great to have known you and to have been part of something worthwhile, something much bigger than any one of us.

7

Up North (London that Is)

We would say we are top dogs in London, West Ham would say that they were as would Tottenham and Millwall. But we can all have a bad day at the office and even Charlton and Palace will give you a run for your money. But I believe we have had more good days than bad and that's what keeps us up there.

However, Tottenham has always been our biggest rival firm-wise and there has always been major hatred between us and the Penny Chews. I hate everything about them: the team, the fans and the area. Having said that, I will admit to rating them as a mob over the years.

If there is one thing that annoys me about them it is that they never tell the truth: to listen to them you would think they won every off and never, ever got run. That is bollocks. We all have bad days and I will admit to being in the Ifield tavern when Spurs came in and wrecked the place. Sometimes, whether you like it or not, you have to give credit where it's due.

One good example of their bullshit is an incident at the Three Kings, which is at the top of North End Road. It has been stated in many football-violence books along the lines of 'Spurs took Chelsea's main boozer'. That is crap. Yes they did get there early – and to be fair with a good mob – but they didn't 'take' it and it certainly wasn't 'our' pub. We heard they were in there and we went along to have it out with them.

When we reached the Three Kings they came to the front door and we could see they were well tooled up with coshes and bottles. We also had bottles and the two mobs were pelting each other with them. No one got to throw a punch because after a few minutes the Old Bill turned up and everyone fucked off. But all you hear from Spurs is how they took a Chelsea pub, but the fact is they didn't throw a single punch and neither did we.

I also remember one in Oxford Street, when Tottenham were in the Argyll. We told them we were coming but for whatever reason I don't think they believed us. As we arrived – well tooled up, I might add – we saw their spotters at the top of the tube station, who immediately warned their pals inside the pub. They came to the doorway and we started throwing things at them, pushing them back inside the pub. It was a tough shift for them. As they emerged our lads whacked them with iron bars and bottles.

That was a great day out but the most brutal violence we inflicted on them was in Parson's Green in the 1990s. It was a game with a 12.45 kickoff and five hours after the final whistle Tottenham were gloating about being in the White Horse, a pub in Parsons Green, which is in the Stamford Bridge area. They would see drinking in a pub in Chelsea's area as a result and as them taking a complete liberty with us. But we've never drunk there so fuck knows what they were on about.

Little did they know we were just down the road, armed to the teeth. An article in the *Evening Standard* from the time shows that we had a fearsome array of weapons including hockey sticks, knives and coshes. Our pièce de résistance was a baseball bat with nails sticking out, a photograph of which the *Standard* was delighted to publish.

When Tottenham came out of the pub we took them by surprise. It was proper, old-school Chelsea. One of their lads got stabbed, others got slashed and the lucky ones were beaten on the head and body by baseball bats. Although some Chelsea got arrested that is an occupational hazard and the lads were happy with their day's work.

But knowing Tottenham, they are probably claiming they won that one – or at least that they did all right. But I can honestly say it was a very good day at the office.

Spurs were also involved in the weirdest, yet the best, away day I have ever had. It was the 1980s, New Year's Day, and we had West Ham away. There was a fucking good mob of us on the Oxo that day and when we got off at Upton Park we walked up to the top of the stairs, where, as usual, the Old Bill were waiting. They told us the game had been cancelled and that we wouldn't be going any further. 'Make your way back home,' they said.

On the other side of the Old Bill lines there was a mob of West Ham. 'Go to Highbury Fields and we will meet you there,' they shouted. We were well up for it and as there were no cozzers wrapped around us it was definitely on.

On our way we realise that Arsenal are playing Tottenham so when we get to Highbury Fields we aren't that surprised when we bump into a mob of Gooners who are obviously looking for Spurs. We end up having a row with Arsenal and do very well although, to be fair, we took them by surprise as they were looking for Tottenham. The Old Bill arrive, round us up and naturally think we are the Penny Chews as we are rowing with Arsenal. So to make the streets safer they march us straight to the ground and put us in the Clock End, which is the away section at Highbury.

So here we are. In the away end at Arsenal along with our biggest rivals, Spurs, who don't have a clue we are in there. To say we were amazed is an understatement.

It is a lot better than playing away at West Ham, any day of the week. We didn't hold it back for long before we let every cunt know exactly who we were and going mental. As I said it is the best away day I have ever had although I wouldn't mind my twelve quid back as I didn't see any of the game, not that I wanted to of course! It wouldn't happen today, not with all the technology and the higher level of football intelligence. So it was one to remember.

I am going to contradict myself again. Despite our many vicious battles with Spurs, and my loathing of everything about the club and their supporters, I do know quite a lot of them personally. In the 1980s Tottenham had a firm called the Richmond Spurs. I went to school with a lot of them and got to know others. They were the days of the Highfield Tavern off, when they came round and did us. I am also very good pals with one of their main faces, Rob Campbell. He is just a real good lad. As I said I am contradicting myself but that's the strange world of football violence for you.

Arsenal, Tottenham's north London rivals, had a good mob in the Eighties. Although they are never the first name on anyone's lips when it comes to football violence, to me they were never given the credit they deserved. More often than not Arsenal were well up for it and have to be respected.

One time I well remember was the first game of the 1984/85 season, the twenty-fifth of August, a very hot sunny day. We gathered in the North London tavern in Kilburn High Road, the pub we always met in before games at White Hart Lane and Highbury. Being a Kilburn boozer there were always a lot of Irish Republican sympathisers knocking about and this was no exception. This cunt was walking around the pub with a tin in his hand, collecting money for the IRA, which was normal for that area.

He got totally abused and told to fuck off. I am aware you need two hands to clap, and that there are two sides to every story, but collecting money for the RAH ain't the right thing to do for Chelsea supporters.

Mobs were so much bigger back then and I would guess we had three hundred-plus out that day. As we marched confidently to the ground the main Old Bill football-intelligence officer, Penfold, came up to me.

'Where are you going?' he demanded.

'I don't know. I am just following the crowd.'

Of course, I knew exactly where I was going.

'If I see you anywhere near their end I will nick you.'

But in those days I didn't give a fuck. I just wanted to get inside that stadium and attack Arsenal. The filth stopped us from getting into the home end, which was still terracing. So we made for the clock end, along with about fifteen thousand other Chelsea. When we got inside we could see there was a good mob of Arsenal there and the skirmishes started almost immediately. Unfortunately, the police – who were by now beginning to get their act together – controlled it easily and chucked the Gooners mob out. Nothing else happened in the ground and the only other thing I can remember is the great Kerry Dixon scoring for us in a 1–1 draw.

A few years later, I arranged a row with Jimmy Sillence, an Arsenal lad, but despite agreeing it all with him we didn't think they would show. They were in the George in Hammersmith so we met up in a pub in Gloucester Road, which is not that far away. After a few drinks we were on the march, heading for the George. Arsenal saw us coming and streamed out. At first we had the upper hand, throwing bottles and running straight at them, backing them off.

But fair play to them, they came right back at us and as we had all run out of missiles fist fights broke out all over the street. As more and more of them came out of the George they began to outnumber us. Eventually, helped by their sheer weight of numbers, they had us on our toes. The last thing I remember was Romford Lee, who was one of us, being surrounded by the law in a chip shop and one of the cops bending down and pulling a tin of CS gas out of a bin. Lee had thrown it in there, hoping he would not be spotted but he was too late and I am afraid to say he got six months for possession of firearms.

8

'Bring Out Your Riot Gear, Cos England's Here'

I always loved going away with England. Apart from being a proud Englishman, it was a great opportunity to cause a bit of mayhem on the Continent. In those days Chelsea were never in Europe and although we always took a good mob to away grounds at home we could never get to strut our stuff abroad. One of my earliest trips was to the 1988 European Championships in West Germany. It really was the old days, prehistoric even: only eight teams in the tournament (yes eight, really, I double-checked it), Germany two years away from reunification and the old Soviet Union still going strong.

England found themselves in Group B, along with the Soviets, Republic of Ireland and Holland. Not much chance of a row with our Russian friends: the poor cunts would be lucky if they were allowed to watch the games on television – black and white, of course. How times have changed. Nor would an off with the Paddies be on the cards because they didn't really go in for that sort of thing. The Dutch, however, were a different kettle of fish. They always had a good mob out and they were always up for it. Our game against them was in Dusseldorf, almost a home fixture for them.

After losing the first game to the Tea Caddies in Stuttgart we made the long journey to Dusseldorf. When I got there England were everywhere and I am not talking about scarfers. At least a thousand hardcore lads were on the streets, every man and his dog ready to get stuck into the Dutch. We swamped the place. It was without doubt the biggest, and best, England mob I had ever seen and we were all together outside the Swordfish bar. For once club rivalries seemed to go out the window, either that or people were avoiding each other on purpose. I have always believed England is the most-feared and respected mob in the world and that when we get our act together there are no gamer kids anywhere. Our only problem would be avoiding the clutches of the Dusseldorf Old Bill, who were out in numbers, most of them in full riot gear.

As kickoff approached the anticipation grew steadily. We kept hearing rumours about what time the German lookalikes might arrive. But the truth is that no one knew for certain. Then we got the shout. 'They're here.' We rushed out into the main square, ready for battle. But it was a non-event, just another fucking rumour. We went back to the Swordfish, and carried on drinking and waiting.

'They're here. They're here.'

I was with Cockney Tony, Disco and Andy Garner. We were outside the bar, and along with hundreds more England we ran to confront the Dutch. Even in their worst nightmare I don't think they would have been expecting what was about to hit them. There were a lot of them, don't get me wrong, but we still outnumbered them. Our tactics were also good because we launched a classic pincer movement, with a splinter group attacking them from the rear.

It worked. We proper gave it to them.

The ones we caught took a lot of punishment and the rest we ran. I had a straightener in the road with a geezer who was a proper unit; think Giant Haystacks and you wouldn't be far away. I certainly wouldn't want his food bill on a Friday afternoon. Despite his height I managed to land one on his jaw and as soon as I connected one of my mates caught him with a flying kick, Bruce Lee style, which was double handy as he would probably have smashed the granny out of me.

They had come in big numbers looking to put one over on England, but on the day there was only going to be one winner. It was a different story on the pitch. We lost the game to a quality Holland team and you will of course remember Marco Van Basten's wonder volley, one of the best goals ever scored.

Copenhagen

When it came to following England it wasn't just competitive games or big tournaments that got me going. I would often travel to friendlies, which is how I found myself in Denmark on 7 June 1989. That trip started with a flight to Hamburg in the company of Tony Covelle, Skitzy, Dennis from St Neots and many more. We chose Hamburg for a pit stop of a couple of nights because it was much cheaper than Copenhagen.

While I was there I bumped into two old pals of mine from when I was growing up: Paul Winter – who, you will remember from the chapter 'The Young Tearaway', is a Penny Chew – and Olly Plate, a Brussels Sprout. After a few beers Paul, Olly and I decided to go for a kebab. We went into a Turkish takeaway where I ended up having a bit of a disagreement with the old 'Gone Berserk' behind the counter. I was trying to tell him that I didn't want chilli sauce on my kebab but, perhaps because of the language barrier, he put it on anyway.

We started arguing and in the end I decided I had had enough of his bollocks. I told him I didn't want the kebab with the fucking chilli sauce on it. He began to get a bit leery in front of his mates behind the jump so I gassed him. I can honestly say it wasn't one of my cleverest moves. The Gone Berserk came round from behind the counter with a knife as long as a milk round.

By the look on his face I knew it wasn't the doner meat he wanted to cut. It was me.

Between me, Paul and Olly we tried to have a little scuffle but the four-foot knife looked like the winner all day long. So it was an early exit for us. Although to be fair to the other two it was me the Turks were interested in.

The next day we went to Hamburg station for the journey to Copenhagen. When we got off the train we bumped into a little mob of Portsmouth, who we had a long history with, none more so than Tony who had once been cut by a 6.57 lad. So of course we had a bit of a row with them before heading for the city centre. By now there are many like-minded people in the pubs and clubs, people we knew from 'up and down the motorway'. Even more drink gets downed before we head for the ground. I would have said there were about a hundred and fifty of us – from many different club mobs – with Chelsea in the vanguard as usual. While we are on the move we are looking for Denmark lads, who are said to be quite tasty and also quite right wing. We also keep our guard up at all times because other nations always want to have a go. On the field everyone wants to play Brazil, simply because they are the best. Off it everyone wants to fight England, where we are the best.

Unfortunately, Denmark don't show up on the way to the game, which means our next chance for FV is at the stadium. The only problem is that none of us have tickets, which means doing the touts or buying one off them. After scouting around we notice that the ticket office is quite small, with very few staff and, even better, no security. We stormed in, grabbed handfuls of tickets and got on our toes before the police arrived.

But the stolen tickets never got used. A decision was made to go into the home end, in the hope of having an off with their mob. We rushed the turnstiles but just as we made our move one of the England lads, Colchester (yes Colchester, he's from that Essex town), decided to tear gas the turnstile attendants. The fucking gas blew back and gassed loads of us. It wafted right into my face: my eyes were streaming and I was coughing and spluttering and struggling to breath.

It turned out that the tear gas was the least of my worries because the next thing I knew an Old Bill had steamed into me. He chored me and took me to Copenhagen nick. Only four people got arrested and silly bollocks me was one of them. We all got put in the same cell: two touts, Salford (who despite his Northern name is Chelsea) and me. The touts weren't there for anything football-related, they had been arrested for grafting tickets for a pop concert.

The only good thing was that I had not been searched before being banged up. It meant the cozzers hadn't found the match ticket in my pocket, which would have put me right in the frame for robbing the office. In England by this stage I would have been searched and the ticket would have been found. However, there was still a problem. I couldn't immediately get rid of the ticket because I had been cuffed and, surely, before long, I was going to be searched.

I was in a tight spot and inside I was panicking. Somehow I had to get rid of that fucking ticket. It was a holding cell with no toilet to flush it away. So the only thing I could do was to eat it, but as it was obviously made of paper I needed water. I pressed the buzzer, asked the Old Bill for a drink and ate the ticket. It tasted horrible and it took ages but anything was better than spending time in the nick.

The touts and I got released after the game but Salford wasn't so lucky. He didn't eat his ticket, which the Old Bill found, and he got four months in a Danish nick. I can honestly say that the tramp had never had it so good.

Italia 90

The Rose and Crown in Rimini, a well-known bar right on the main drag that runs alongside the sea front. It pulls up its shutters during the times it is serving, creating a huge open-plan space from which you could see not only the busy road but also the beach. I started drinking in there at two in the afternoon and people were coming and going the whole day long. At its peak I would say there were five hundred England in the place, game lads from all over the country. The atmosphere was good, very boisterous, with many more stood outside and everyone waiting for the Italy versus Czechoslovakia game later that night.

We were in Italy so we wanted Italy to lose. Simple as that. But they didn't, they won two–nil, prompting their fans to drive up and down the street outside the bar, waving their flags out the windows, standing up through their sun roofs, chanting 'Italia Italia' and generally going mental like Italians always do. Did that annoy us? To a certain extent, but we didn't need an excuse. We started to abuse them, 'fuck off you cunts', we were shouting. It might have stayed that way, with the verbals, but as I knew only too well it only takes one man to spark a battle.

And that's what happened. One of our lads threw a pint glass at a carful of Italians and within seconds hundreds of England were volleying glasses, chairs and tables in the general direction of their convoy. It got very nasty, very quickly, and I remember thinking this could easily turn into a proper riot. There were very few police about but when they pulled their batons out they also got pelted with glasses and ashtrays.

By now everyone is outside the Rose and Crown. It goes ballistic and we waded into both the Old Bill and the Italian fans. Anyone and everyone who weren't England were getting it and getting it big time. We hear the wails of police sirens in the distance but we are fuelled up after eight hours of solid drinking and do not give a fuck. As police reinforcements arrive there is a lot of charging back and forwards with some cozzers pounding us with batons and others taking off their thick white belts and lashing us.

With so many of them now on the scene the *carabinieri*, or whatever the fuck they're called over there, pushed some of us down the street and away from the bar while the rest of us, me included, got forced onto the terrace and into the Rose and Crown interior. As we retreat we are still hurling missiles but rapidly running out of ammunition. I have been in many battles, home and abroad, but take it from me this was a fucking good 'un. To show them that we weren't going to back down we started singing them a little song:

'Bring out your riot gear,
Cos England's here, England's here'

I don't know if that was the straw that broke the camel's whatsitface or not but, by this time, they had had more than enough. All of a sudden a big metal ball hits the ceiling of the Rose and Crown and falls on the floor with a dull thud. 'Fucking tear gas,' someone shouted and as soon as the words left his lips the gas started to seep out. If it had been hairy before that, the danger levels now went up by several notches. In fact it was complete chaos and complete madness. Many of the lads panicked; a natural reaction in a crowded room thick with tear gas. Some blokes knew what to do, others didn't. In fact, the worst thing you can do is to rub your eyes. I took my T-shirt off and put it over my nose and mouth.

I had been in many tight spots before so I kept my head, which enabled me to clock everything that was going on. I noticed the staff had fucked off from behind the bar as soon as the trouble started, leaving the till unattended. Because of the amount of drink we had bought, it was full of cash. My natural reaction, it was almost instinctive, was to jump the bar and help myself to the pie and mash. I stuffed my pockets full of notes, a nice little earner, which helped pay for my trip. I don't have time to feel guilty about it but I would like to take this opportunity of apologising to my mates: after all, they had spent good money that day and here I was helping myself to the takings.

The police rounded us up and took us outside where we were forced to lie on the ground, face down. Not content with calling us 'English pigs' and 'hooligans' they started to kick us. Eventually, they put plastic hand-cuffs round our wrists before shepherding us into vans. No less than 247 England got deported that night on a special plane, without luggage, and when we got home we could have written the 'Scum' headlines ourselves.

The next day England won 1–0; thanks to a quality free kick from Gazza, which led to an equally good finish from David Platt.

Another great memory of that tournament is being out there with my lifelong pal, Darren Crewe, who we have just lost to cancer. I am gutted. I loved that man.

The Poles

Since 1973 we have met Poland fifteen times in competitive matches. It became almost like a domestic league fixture we saw so much of them. The Poles now have a tasty reputation as hooligans but back in the day they weren't known for it. That changed in 1989 after a game in Katowice, at which many England fans were assaulted. So we knew that when we went back there in November 1991 for a European Championship qualifier the chances of it kicking off were pretty good.

As we often did with England we did a bit of sightseeing along the way. I hired a car and drove over with just three of us in a seven-seater, which left enough room to kip down in case we couldn't get a bed for the night. Our first stop was Berlin where we had arranged to meet up with TC, Fat pat and a few of the other Chelsea herberts. One thing will always stick in my mind from that trip.

It was the day I met a genuine, 100 per cent superstar.

On a visit to Checkpoint Charlie one of the lads, Trav – who is actually a Man City fan – thought he recognised a fellow sightseer.

'Fuck me. Is that Johnny Cash over there?'

I had a look and, stone me, it really was the Man in Black.

'Do you know what? I think it is,' I replied.

I couldn't resist it. I go walking across the street and had a word with him.

'All right, Johnny. How are you mate?'

I was half-expecting him to look at me like a cunt, wondering what the fuck I was on about. But to my surprise he turned round and said:

'Yeah, man, not too bad.'

I was well happy by now; after all the man is a legend. I asked him if it was okay to have a photograph taken with him and he was as good as gold. After it was taken, he had a question for me.

'How did you recognise me?'

I was on a roll now and, with a laugh, I explained.

'Well, you know what, Johnny. It's minus forty-seven out here, and there ain't a lot of penny-in-the-banks walking about with open black shirts on with big medallions. So it was quite a giveaway.'

By the next day more and more England were arriving in Berlin. The Old Bill were all around us and it became obvious that quite a few of the football-intelligence lot were among them. We knew that because there were well-known faces with us we would be closely watched from now on.

We holed up in two bars during which time some of the lads went and did some of the armoury shops. Before long we were well tooled up with tear gas and the like. It's as easy to get that gear over there as it is to buy a Mars Bar in England. As the beer began to take its toll the mood changed. The German cozzers knew we were on our way to Poland, but they didn't know we weren't going that night, so they tried to move us on. Of course we didn't want to be moved and it kicked off big time. We steamed into the Old Bill, the tear gas goes off; the bars get smashed up, the papers have something to write about.

Par for the course when you go away with England.

The next day we arrived in Poznan. That night we expected to have it with the Poles but we saw no sign of them. People kept saying, 'Don't worry they will be here. Just give them time.' But nothing.

So we went on a bit of a pub crawl, meeting different people, and after a full day on the drink I ended up going to bed at some crazy hour in the morning.

I couldn't have been asleep for long when there was a knock on my door. I woke up and heard everyone shouting, 'They're here. They're here.'

'Who's fucking here?' I asked.

One of the lads burst into my room.

'The Polish. Seriously, they are fucking here.'

I looked at my watch.

'Don't be fucking ridiculous. It's half-past eight in the morning.'

But he was right. It turned out that about twenty-five England had been sitting in the restaurant downstairs, some of them having breakfast, some still drinking from the night before, when a huge mob of Poles came bouncing in and attacked them. I looked out of the window and saw about 150 of them outside the hotel. I thought to myself: 'What time do they set their alarms for? It's half-eight in the morning.'

By now it was like a Laurel and Hardy sketch. Everyone knocking on everyone else's door, people running down the corridor trying to put on their clothes, others falling over when they put both feet into the same trouser leg, jumpers on back to front.

We got outside and mobbed up and got a close look at them for the first time. I wasn't impressed. Scruffy skinheads in tight denim jeans, mad trainers and loud tracksuit tops. They must have a few quid because they spend fuck all on clothes. But at least they had shown up and called it on.

We really got our act together, which, when you have been on the piss until four in the morning, is a real achievement. As soon as we ran at them they didn't want to know. They were happy bullying twenty-five or so lads eating bacon and eggs or drinking vodka and orange but when they came up against us they soon found out who the guvnors were.

The day of the game, after a few beers, thirty of us went on a walkabout and crossed over a dual carriageway that took you down into a railway station. There was a group of about thirty Polish in the station and knowing that it's easier to fight going downwards we piled down the stairs towards them. I'll give them credit: they came to meet us and although we kicked them back down the stairs they wanted it as much as we did.

We went back to the bar and about an hour-and-a-half before kickoff we were on the march. A firm somewhere between three and four hundred, all top lads. It was a fair old walk and we had the Old Bill keeping tabs on us, but it wasn't a tight escort at first and the Poles had a few opportunities to come at us from the side streets. But they didn't want it enough. We surged towards them every time we laid eyes on them but they back-pedalled straight away.

As we got closer to the ground the cozzers got their act together. A line of Old Bill three-deep – fully equipped with tear gas, riot helmets and truncheons – kept the two mobs apart. Then, just before we got to the stadium, we went past a tram-load of them. There were about forty Polish in each carriage, singing and shouting and giving us the big 'un. Unlucky for them they stopped right next to the cream of our firm and when the doors slid open we ran onto the tram and hauled them off.

Not only did we kick fuck out of them but we also gassed the cunts. The Chelsea contingent had bought swimming goggles to protect them from the CS gas and we had a mad photo taken that would go down well in a Headhunters family album.

Inside the stadium the Poles seemed content to knock seven bells out of each other. We watched as they battled non-stop and then after the game we were well wrapped up by the Old Bill. It was a moody place but I had every confidence in that England firm. In those days the right people followed England, unlike today when someone pulls on a Stone Island jumper and thinks he can have a row. That day I would say that 80 per cent of the away support were hooligans. No firm could have lived with us.

We were back in Poland two years later and then in 1997, when I went with my old mate Andy 'Nightmare' Frain. This time we were in Chorzow, where there is fuck all to do apart from drink. Two nights before the game we were in a bar that had been taken over by England and we spent the night drinking with Lee Spence from Oldham and his pals. We expected trouble from the Poles but it seemed they only turned out on the day of the game so we had no problems at all that night.

Even on match-day it didn't really go off. There were a few running battles but nothing to write home about, not when you had been involved in the scene for as long as we had. What sticks in my mind is the Polish Old Bill. They made me chuckle: you would see them unshaven, in a bar and having a quick fag while on duty. They are not interested in giving you a speeding ticket but they liked a bit of football violence because, like me, they just wanted to hit some cunt because there's fuck all else happening. And hit us they did, but I'm not complaining because we gave them good reason to give us a few clumps with their batons.

But the most memorable thing on that trip was a little drive Andy and I took the day before the game. We had decided to lay off the drink mainly because we didn't want to have a hangover for the main event. So we were looking for something to do when we found out that Auschwitz was only an hour away by taxi. I'm not being funny but if you go to Paris you will want to see the fucking Eiffel Tower, just because it's historically important. So is Auschwitz, which is also the biggest tourist attraction in that part of the world.

The cab driver had obviously done it a million times before and he even came in to show us around. It was an eerie place, very quiet; you would have heard a pin drop. I learnt a lot that day: as you walked through the gates there was a sign that read *arbeit macht frei*, or, in English, work brings freedom. It was a ringer, a moody blag: the inmates would go in there, work their bollocks off and then wind up in the gas chambers. When we got back home and told people about it only being an hour away they said we would have been mad not to have had a look at a proper bit of history. That was how Andy and I felt too.

Little did we know that our excursion to Auschwitz would come back to haunt us.

9

A Good Twenty-Seven Though

It was 15 April 1989. The day of the greatest tragedy in the history of English football. That was when ninety-six Liverpool fans died in the Hillsborough disaster. It was one of those Twin Towers moments, when everyone remembers where they were when they heard the news. I have my own reason for remembering that day: I got nicked for fighting at Leicester and was detained for the weekend, pending a court appearance.

I must say the custodial arrangements could have been better. I walked into the cell and discovered that I was banged up with was the fella I had been fighting with. Maybe the Old Bill were having a laugh. I went back and forth to the magistrates court three times before, on the Monday morning, I was given a fine.

But then we always seemed to have it when we went up to Leicester. For reasons that are not clear to me Chelsea and the Baby Squad have been massive rivals for years. No one knows why. It has always been that way. I suppose it is a compliment for both mobs: if someone hates you, and you hate them, you must be doing something right.

In fact one of the best offs we have ever had was Leicester away. It was 6 May 1994 and we turned out a good couple of hundred that day. To throw the Old Bill off the scent, the plan was to go one stop on the train past Leicester, to Loughborough, and meet up in a pub called the Railway, around eleven. After a good few beers most of the lads decided to go to the game, but twenty-seven of us decided to stay in the pub and I know it was twenty-seven because my pal Muzza decided to do a head-count. Very precise was our Muzza.

I couldn't miss the opportunity to take the piss.

'Not twenty-five of us, not thirty. Twenty-seven. Are you sure you got that one right Muzz?'

'Yes Jason. Twenty-seven.'

I smiled at him.

'Yeah, Muzza. But it ain't half a good fucking twenty-seven.'

And it was. As well as Muzza and me, they were all top boys: Nightmare, Nick from Bromley (who is now deceased, RIP mate), Tony Covelle, Perky, Dave and Ian Sim.

It was the last game of the season and we were desperate to get to grips with Leicester's mob. We had been in touch with the bigger Chelsea contingent inside the stadium to get the SP on what had been happening. Unfortunately, we didn't have a clue if we were coming back to Loughborough or not.

By this time we had all had a skinful. There was no way we were going back to London without looking for the enemy.

'Fuck it,' we thought, 'we'll go to their town centre.'

So we marched out of the pub and got on a train for Leicester town centre. When we arrived we came out of the station and walked, diagonally, across the road.

Then, in the distance, we saw them. There didn't seem to be that many of them. Maybe twenty-seven would be enough. Would it fuck.

As we drew closer we could see their mob was getting bigger and bigger. There must have been a hundred and fifty of the cunts. We were outnumbered six-to-one on our opponents' manor. Not a great prospect you might think and you couldn't have blamed us for having it away on our toes. But it didn't enter our heads to run.

Why?

We were full of drink.

We were twenty-seven of the gamest lads you have ever met.

And most important of all, we fucking hate Leicester.

'Stand Chelsea. Stand Chelsea.'

It was all you could hear, twenty-seven voices in unison.

All of a sudden there was an almighty roar. I turned round and got the shock of my life. There from the other end of the street, from behind us, another eighty Baby Squad were coming our way. There was a deafening silence. Not one of our boys uttered a sound. Without saying a word we had taken a collective decision: this was now a suicide mission. We had to have it on our Bromleys.

Just as we started to leg it, the Old Bill turned up. If I'm being honest, I had never been so pleased to see them in my life. With the twenty-seven now broken up into even smaller units I found myself in a group of just eight, which was being pointed in the direction of the station by the cozzers.

As we approached I noticed a group crossing the bridge and heading for our platform. It was Leicester.

'There's a mob coming over the bridge,' I shouted.

And that's when it kicked off. Fifteen or so Baby Squad against eight of us. It was a really good toe-to-toe. Nick from Bromley tried his best to kung-fu kick one of theirs but landed right on his arse. That was hilarious but what wasn't funny was how narrow that platform was. As I was fighting the thought kept going through my mind; what if these cunts get the better of me and I end up on the tracks. I didn't have the slightest doubt that they would do it; the hatred between the two clubs was just so intense.

We did well on the platform against Leicester. Then the Old Bill came on the scene and started whacking everyone with their truncheons. I remember turning round and seeing that Dave the twin had rugby tackled an Old Bill, desperately trying to pull himself up after a fight with one of the Baby Squad. Some of us had taken a good few blows from the cozzers, as well as fighting with Leicester.

The arrival of the law was too late to save Dave's twin, Ian, from being cut by a big black fella on the back of his neck. An ambulance arrived and Ian was taken to hospital, accompanied by Dave. Leicester were still milling about outside and tried to attack the ambulance because the twins were inside.

We later found out that forty Baby Squad had come to the railway pub to have it with us but that we had just missed them. I would have preferred that to what actually happened because the numbers would have been more evenly balanced. Still, I think Leicester have to respect what we did that day. Not many firms would march into the middle of Leicester prepared to take on the massed ranks of the Baby Squad at six-thirty in the evening. And with only Muzza's gallant twenty-seven in tow.

Incidentally, I am now pals with a few of Leicester's mob, especially Coalville Daz (Smith), who is a really good friend through organising an after-dinner talk for me up in Coalville. To be fair, they're good lads.

10

A Normal Day Out with the Lads

Awaydays with the lads were always special, no matter who we were playing. In the Eighties we always met in the pub early on the Saturday morning to get our coach. The boozer wasn't officially open at that time but we slipped in through the back door. We had the place boxed off so we would wash down a sausage roll with a pint of cold lager before heading for the M25.

For argument's sake if we were playing in Manchester, we would leave the pub at eight o'clock. The atmosphere on the bus was always good with plenty of banter and everyone taking the piss out of everyone else. Some people would have a game of cards, others would talk bollocks and have a good laugh. On the way up there would be people practising their favourite vice: smoking, drinking, taking drugs or even all three at once.

To me football was a very small part of it. It was about the whole day. You never knew what was going to happen because every away game was different. That said we are all creatures of habit so if we were playing in Manchester or Liverpool nine times out of ten we would stop off at Watford Gap services. To this day I want to know why it's called *Watford* Gap. Because it's in the opposite direction to Watford and it's actually closer to Birmingham than it is to Watford. The prices there, like in all motorway service stations, are extortionate. I think the reason is that when coach-loads like ours went into one we would rob it fucking blind.

On the way up we would always run into Chelsea coaches and because there were forty-six other league games on the chances were we would also meet mobs from other clubs. Depending on the mob it could kick right off. There were many such rows but one that sticks in my mind is the day we bumped into a load of Pompey, who were always well up for it. Fuck knows how it started but it did. I remember us all going toe to-toe inside the services and then as it moved outside things really escalated in the car park. It was a good row that lasted for three minutes, although at the time it seemed like ten.

Although lads on both sides got weighed in no one got seriously hurt. There are always cozzers at the service stations and they arrived and broke it up. Maybe we felt a bit restrained in the services because even in the 1980s we knew they were camerad-up and so we had to be very careful. It was something that was always in the back of your mind. But it was a starter for the main course if you get my drift. After the off with Portsmouth had finished we went on our way as if nothing had happened.

Arriving in the host city could also be memorable. Many a time the coach would get attacked with cunts throwing bricks at the windows. It was all part and parcel of the day. I recall driving away from Goodison Park and I had my head against the window. We got bricked by the Scousers. I've still got a headache from it but lucky for me the windows were very hard to put through. That was the famous day we beat Everton 4–3 with Gordon Davies scoring a hat trick. He never played for the club again.

There were times when we took tools with us on the coach. You might carry something you normally wouldn't if you were going up against a mob you were likely to have a row with. But you could never be sure what was going to happen in those days. Football then was unpredictable. There was no internet and no mobile phones so when you turned a corner you had no idea what you would be facing.

My little part trick was a Vick's bottle filled with Olbas oil (it is for colds) that you could buy over the counter in the chemist. In my opinion it was better than gas because it doesn't blind them but it does sting your eyes meaning that you are temporarily blind. It was also handy when the cozzers started to search coaches as a matter of routine after drink was banned. If they saw the nasal spray I would say I had a cold and there was nothing they could do.

No matter how good the journey and the banter, the main course on the awayday was taking on opposition mobs in their own backyard. One I always remember was a night game at Stoke around 1993. We have a healthy rivalry with the Naughty Forty and there is, if I'm being honest, mutual respect between the two mobs. So we knew there was always a good chance that something would go off up there.

Fifteen of us travelled in a minibus and got off at Hanley, which is in the heart of their manor. We met up with a coachload of our mates and then walked to the ground. Nothing happened before or during the game but when we came out you could sense the atmosphere. There were groups of Stoke everywhere, all of them looking for Chelsea. We walked back to our minibus, which was parked near to a bus station.

That was when Stoke showed their hand.

A mob of them came towards us and as they closed in one of them – I now know it was Jasper (Mark Chester) – fired a flare. Lucky for us, and unlucky for them, it hit the canopy of a shop and bounced back onto them, which could obviously have done them some damage. It was just the start. There were skirmishes all over the place that night, right up until ten o'clock. When it was all over we got back on our bus and on the way back we stopped off in Wolverhampton, where, for some, reason we picked up a Fulham fan and gave him a lift back to London.

Stoke is another good example of me making friends with a fierce rival. Mark Chester – the author of *Naughty: the Story of a Football Hooligan Gang* – and I are now good pals.

In terms of the numbers who travelled one of the biggest days out in Chelsea history came when we played Grimsby on the last day of season 1983/84. We had to win to go up as champions and naturally we took an army: there must have been ten thousand Chelsea there. The day was full of excitement from the minute we got on the coach, which was full of the usual herberts. The likes of Darren Crewe, Andy Bedwood, Richard Saxford, Peter and Graham Russell and John Mapletoft were there; all hoping to see us win the title.

It was a long journey and I remember that the air vents were open most of the way. We didn't need to be told when we had reached Grimsby: the smell of fish pouring through the vents made it all too fucking obvious! The few miles from the edge of town to the ground were amazing. Every other person on the streets was Chelsea. I have never seen a town taken over so much in my life. We were fucking everywhere. We were singing and banging the windows, getting carried away with ourselves.

We eventually get off the coach, carrying our lager, drinking, and singing; letting every cunt know Chelsea was here. It was our biggest game yet and we were going to enjoy it. There were mobs of Grimsby around but we were too overpowering. They wouldn't have had a chance.

Eventually we get into the stadium. I was behind the goals in the away end, but Chelsea were in all four parts of the ground. The whole place was very overcrowded with people even spilling onto the pitch at times. In our end alone there were over a thousand without tickets. I expected a day of celebration without any trouble but I got that one totally wrong. Grimsby had a right fucking go. There were fights before, during and after the game and inside the stadium; the only place there wasn't any trouble was in our end. With our weight of numbers we took the honours but, fair play to them, they wanted an off.

And yes we won, one-nil, and went up to the first division as champions, thanks to a goal from the one and only Kerry Dixon.

What a day!

11

England: the Later Years

I flew straight into Amsterdam the day before the game. There were mobs
and mobs of England about, most of them hanging about the red-light
area and the streets adjacent to the famous canals. The numbers were
ridiculous but the team was playing Holland in a vital World Cup qualifier:
win, or even draw, and we would go to USA 1994; lose and we were out.
The Dutch also had a big, and growing, reputation for football violence
and when you threw in the attractions of downtown Amsterdam I probably
shouldn't have been surprised by the numbers who travelled.

The problem that night was that the Dutch Old Bill got heavy-handed
with the English fans. I bet they wish they hadn't bothered because, within
minutes, a mass brawl had kicked off. As well as attacking the police we
smashed shop windows, threw bikes into the canals, overturned cars. You
can buy tear gas legally in Holland so, guess what, we did and we weren't
slow to use it on the Old Bill. It was total fucking mayhem but it turned out
to be the calm before the storm.

The next morning we had time to kill. Lots of it. Those who liked weed
were happily smoking it in the 'coffee shops' and pubs, people who liked
drinking were drinking, those who liked both were doing both. Eventually,
we boarded the train for Rotterdam, where the game was being played,
every single one of us drunk, stoned or a bit of both. There were English
football-intelligence officers on the train and they were busy identifying
us and pointing us out to their Dutch counterparts. I don't speak Dutch
but I got the gist of it all right.

When we got off the train there were a good five hundred game lads
all well up for it. We thought we would have to go looking for the Dutch
but they came right at us the minute we got out of the station. These cunts

weren't there to shout abuse at us behind police lines either because the first thing we knew they launched a missile.

It was a nail bomb, which went off with a hell of a bang, driving metal splinters into the flesh of some of our lads. This was going to be some party!

We had quite an arsenal of our own. One of the boys fired a flare gun at them; others set off smoke bombs. We steamed in, angered by the nail bomb and fuelled by adrenalin, hash and alcohol, a dangerous combination. There were toe-to-toes going off all over the shop and despite being outnumbered we were more than holding our own. As you can imagine the Old Bill were there in huge numbers and they waded in, separating the two mobs.

The police also had snatch squads and what one of them did makes me laugh to this day. Tony Covelle got snatched and he was dragged into the back of a police van, where he got strip-searched. Then, incredibly, the Old Bill threw him out – right in the middle of the Dutch mob. Tony managed to keep his head down and slipped away.

Once that off had died down we had to get another train to the stadium. Loads of us made it and we were well up for round two either outside or inside the ground. Unfortunately, as soon as we stepped onto the platform, the Dutch police grabbed me and hauled me to off to a specially made cage outside the ground. Before long I was joined by many more known faces and none of us got to see the game.

That was the infamous match during which Graham Taylor was heard uttering the meaningless phrase 'Do I not like that,' a remark that he has never been allowed to forget. All I can say, Graham my old mate, is that I knew what you meant. Arrested, held in a cage, missing the game, England out of the World Cup. 'Do I not like that.' It summed my day up perfectly. I've not seen the game to this day.

World Cup 1998

The World Cup was next door, in France. With it being so easy to get to everyone wanted to go whether they were a straight member or a known face. The problem was that every cop in England and in France was equally determined to stop us getting there. Their technology, systems and organisation had vastly improved over the years so we knew it would be far from easy to evade their clutches. Airports, railway stations and ports; the Old Bill would be watching like hawks for Category, A, B and

C lads like me and my pals. We would be lucky to get any further than the Dartford crossing on the M25.

I racked my brains and came up with what I thought was a very cunning plan. I bought an old campervan and went to the considerable trouble of registering it in Ireland, which enabled me to fit it with Irish number plates. I set off with Steve King, Levy and a couple of others.

Sure enough when we get to Calais there are untold Old Bill at the passport checks, along with spotters. While the cars from other countries get waved through all the English cars are getting pulled over and checked. As the campervan had foreign plates we also got waved through, right up to passport control. But one of the English football-intelligence cunts was wide awake that day. He recognised me and waved to the French cops at passport control to stop the van. But he was a fraction of a second too late. We were through and into France. My plan had worked and, as we drove off, I smiled and waved at the cozzers.

We had come over to watch England play Argentina in the quarter-final of the World Cup. The game was in St Etienne, which is a long way from Calais. I decide the best way is to go by train and so I leave the campervan behind and, with Stockport Andy Garner in tow, we head south. Naturally, the journey down there didn't cost us a penny, or, this being France, a cent. When the guard came round – which he did several times – we fucked him about, either pretending we didn't understand French or hiding in the toilet.

Our next requirement was to get a ticket, which was proving to be a very hard task. We milled about all day looking for touts to buy from, or, if it came to it, to rob. After drawing a blank we were outside a bar in St Etienne when Turkish touts came up and asked for £300 a ticket. The touts were in large groups as English lads kept robbing them of their tickets. Andy and I chased them all over the place trying to nick their tickets off them but because there were so many of them we got nowhere. Maybe we would be luckier at the ground.

There was a ring of steel around the stadium; hundreds of police and stewards checking everyone's tickets, much stricter security than I have seen anywhere else. I remember Andy explaining in that Northern accent of his: 'I have to pick my ticket up from the other side,' but the Old Bill either wasn't interested or he couldn't understand a word that Andy was saying. The language barrier actually helped me: while the cozzer and Andy were failing spectacularly to communicate I saw my chance and slipped through the cordon. I wandered off, my body language telling the Old Bill that I don't want or expect them to call me back. To my amazement, half an hour later, I run into Andy, who has somehow managed to get through as well.

'We've slipped through the Old Bill,' we say as we give each other a hug.

Despite our joy there is still one problem: we don't have a ticket. There are no touts around, as they wouldn't, or couldn't, go through the cordon. We have fucked ourselves. We don't know what to do. Our desperation to see the game draws us towards the stadium where we discover that other England fans with no tickets, not many but enough, have also got through the ring of steel. We get into a conversation with some Scousers and Brummies and I say to them, 'We have to get in. We have no alternative but to jump the turnstiles.'

This, after all, is the quarter-final of the World Cup.

I jump the turnstile as it is only waist-high. To our amazement quite a few of the lads get in. Safely inside, I immediately do a runner, blending in with the rest of the crowd. Andy also gets in, by which time both of us are buzzing. Time for a drink and something to eat. They weren't selling alcohol at the kiosk but I order juice, food and cigarettes. Cigarettes! 'You don't even smoke,' Andy says. As the kiosk geezer starts passing me the items I hand them onto Andy, who just looks at me.

I smile at him and say, 'Fuck it. We bunked the train fare. We bunked into the ground. We might as well have these for nothing as well.'

In terms of FV I am sad to say nothing went off. The fans were mixed around the ground, with Argentinians in our end. When they scored me and Andy took it upon ourselves to rip their flag down from a fence, expecting them to come and have a go. But, to our disappointment, they didn't even try to defend their flag.

12

Dawn Raid

Quarter to six in the morning. I'm not a milkman or a postman so I was at home, in my kip, knocking out the zeds. All of a sudden there was a loud thud. What the fuck was that? You ain't at your best at that time so it took me a few seconds to work out what had happened. Then I realised: the Old Bill had just battered my front door off its hinges. Whatever happened to the polite knock?

The TSG cozzers came screaming up the stairs and into my bedroom. I was surrounded by six of the mongrels, all of them dressed in boiler suits and crash helmets, and while one of them informed me they had a search warrant, his mates caused a lot of commotion as they searched other rooms. I told them they shouldn't be doing that without me there in case they planted anything. Their reason for being there, they told me, was that they were looking for tickets for the 1996 Euro Championships, which were being held in England.

I knew the tickets story was just that, a story. They were desperate to take out the main players in advance of the Euros and had got their warrant by claiming, falsely, that I was a ticket tout. The amount of effort they were putting into the operation was considerable: as well as the boiler suits there were plain-clothes Old Bill there to nick me, not to mention their sniffer dog, which was a spaniel, the usual breed used in these raids.

Being raided and having your drum searched is not a nice feeling, made worse because they always have the element of surprise. But it had happened to me so many times before, so I just thought: 'Get on with your fucking search.' On this occasion my conscience was clear because all they would find was £4,000-worth of genuine clothes I was selling. But when they found the clothes they immediately thought they had something on me.

It was all expensive stuff, the top labels: Armani, Stone Island, CP Company. To their way of thinking the clothes had to be stolen. In actual fact I had bought the lot from a mate of mine, a wholesaler, so the gear was definitely 'six and eight'. The only 'nause' was that I would have to prove they were straight.

In the meantime I was nicked and taken to Fulham police station, where as usual I remained completely silent, and I mean completely silent. To me, even a 'no comment' is breaking your silence. My solicitor has done fifteen years of police-cell interviews and he always says to me that I am the only one of his clients who has remained completely silent.

I was able to produce receipts for the clothes, so after all that effort the cozzers had no option but to turn me loose. Their raid was a waste of time and they didn't manage to get a football ban on me for the Euros. It was part of a huge police operation, in which doors up and down the country were broken down, with known lads targeted, searched and questioned. The Old Bill won some and they lost some.

* * *

Talking about occupational hazards, I was away on business, in China as it happens, when I suddenly realised that Chelsea were playing abroad. I was on a football ban at the time and it dawned on me that I had neither handed my passport in, nor had I signed in at a police station. I was six thousand miles away so the chances of doing either were non-existent.

But I had to do something.

So at the earliest opportunity, after phoning my brief, I faxed my flight details to the special office that deals with football-banning orders to prove I was out of the country. After that I left everything in my solicitor's hands and got on with business. I wasn't going to drive myself mad. I didn't even know Chelsea were playing that night. It had been a genuine mistake. In fact being that far from home I didn't even know what day of the week it was, never mind that Chelsea had a game. It was only when I walked past a pub (called the Elephant and Castle, would you believe) and saw that they were showing the game that it dawned on me.

On the fourteen-hour flight back from China, I felt that I had boxed everything off at my end and that there was nothing more I could do. But none of that mattered to the Old Bill. As we were taxiing in to the terminal building at Heathrow a voice came over the public-address system: 'Could

Jason Marriner, in seat 86c, stay seated?' I knew the score. It was obvious I was going to be arrested for breaching my football-banning order. You didn't have to be Columbo to work that one out.

When the plane had come to a standstill they didn't let anyone off, but they did let uniformed Old Bill on to arrest me. The way the other passengers were looking at me you would have thought I was a mass murderer. I wasn't concerned. It was all about a petty football ban. Then I saw three cozzers striding up the aisle, two big units and one short, stocky mongrel with an obvious chip on his shoulder, probably due to his size and shape.

'We need to speak to you about an incident. We will tell you more about it down at the station,' one of the units told me. I knew they had only come on to arrest me and would then be handing me over to officers who dealt with football-related issues.

'No problem,' I replied.

By this time I was already on the phone to my brief and so I passed the phone to them and asked: 'Would you like to speak to my solicitor?'

The units were okay but the short fat cunt was getting agitated. Whether that was because he looked out of place next to his two big mates, or I had annoyed him by handing over the phone, I have no idea. But it gave me the chance to have a bit of fun.

'Oi, little legs. Do us a favour. You couldn't get my hand luggage down and carry it off for me?'

I'll never forget the look on his face. He wasn't happy but it made me chuckle and even the two units started laughing.

Having phoned my solicitor I was just waiting for him to turn up at Heathrow, which he eventually did. He came into my cell and explained to me what I was going to be charged with, which was something like not complying with my football-banning order. I was then charged and given a court date.

I went to court hoping that it would be a straightforward case and that common sense would prevail. I explained to the three 'divs' on the bench (otherwise known as magistrates) that I had no idea Chelsea were playing away that night. I was away on business I told them and at the tail end of my ten-year football ban. During that time I had never failed, until now, to either hand in my passport or to sign on at a police station at the appropriate times. I also proved that I had faxed the details of my flight to my solicitor to prove where I was and that he had logged conversations with me.

After a lot of whispering (and probably playing with each other under the bench) they found me guilty, gave me a fine and another punishment. I was fuming.

'I have made a genuine mistake and I have proved the facts to you. It is blatantly obvious that I am not lying.'

The head magistrate ignored my protest and wanted to know if I was willing to pay anything here and now.

'I am not willing to pay anything today, tomorrow or in eight months' time. Let's not waste anybody's time now. If I was you, I'd get a warrant out for me now as I will be going to prison for this offence,' I told him.

I then had a heated argument with him and, as I walked out of the court, I had a few choice words for him and the two other stooges.

'You ain't even a judge. You're probably a chiropodist. You're a sweet-shop owner. And you work in a chemist.'

That's what I think of them: wannabe, pretend judges.

As I was walking out of court a lady came up and asked me to calm down. She seemed to understand my frustration. She worked in the courts but I am not sure in which department. I told her I wanted to appeal and she was very helpful, which led to me getting my appeal heard in the Crown Court.

In that case the prosecution showed the common sense that, to me, the magistrates had lacked. The prosecuting barrister actually got up and told the judge that the facts I had given to the magistrates were true and that bringing the case against me had been a waste of the taxpayers' time and money. The judge agreed and threw out the case. Quite right too, I thought. After it was over the prosecutor apologised to me and I thanked him for the way he had worded his remarks to the judge. He had played a major part in the success of my appeal.

Just a thought for your consideration. The way the system is supposed to work is like this: you get caught for something, tried, sentenced and then do your time. After that you are free to do what the fuck you like. That doesn't apply to us lads: get convicted of a football-related offence and it carries on even when you come out of the nick. It's ridiculous. Have you ever heard of a burglar being told he can't walk past people's houses? As I write, I still have five years on my football ban, which doesn't expire until 2019. Hazard, Oscar and Fabregas will be at the veteran stage of their careers by then and Mourinho will be manager of Portugal!

If you look at the someone like Max Clifford – who has made a living out of other people's misery – he got eight years for being a nonce and I got six years. Under the rules of the criminal-justice system that means he will do a year more than me. I also find it strange that the newspapers don't go on and on about him. No doubt he is still pulling strings, and rubbing shoulders with journalists, while serving his sentence in a nick called Littlehey in Huntingdon.

In Littlehey – which is 85 per cent made up of sex offenders – you have to sign a form when you go in making a commitment not to call anyone a nonce. If this commitment is breached you get shipped out straight away. Let's put it this way, he is not going to get attacked in there. This will enable him to feel safe and secure because he's mainly with like-minded people.

13

The Hate Bus

It was 1994. FA Cup-final day. And not just any cup-final, but a final against the biggest club in the land. Man United were our opponents and we knew they would bring an enormous mob with them. Our job was to match them not just in terms of size but also in our organisation, which would have to be spot on if we were to avoid the long arm of the law.

We had a long history with United. As two of the leading mobs – and clubs – in the country we have often clashed. Down the years there have been broken bones and slashed faces on both sides so motivation has never been a problem.

This article is from the *Daily Mirror* in September 1977. The paper describes what happened in the bar of the Royal Crown hotel near Manchester airport after a United–Chelsea game.

> Staff and customers fled in terror as 100 rampaging thugs laid into each other with bottles, glasses and pieces of furniture. Damage totalled more than £1,000. Fifty people were taken to hospital and one Manchester man suffered a fractured skull. The vicious brawl erupted late on Saturday night as Chelsea fans celebrated their 1–0 win over United . . . Thirteen windows, twelve chairs and six stools were smashed as fighting spilled out into the car park. Police held forty-nine fans overnight.

Fifty taken to hospital . . . one Manchester man suffered a fractured skull . . . police held forty-nine fans overnight (with several Chelsea sent to Strangeways). Quite a battle and it showed the hatred between us. So we saw the cup final as a chance to have another pop at the Men in Black. The problem, as ever, was outwitting the Old Bill.

I had an idea. We knew the filth would be on the ball. 'So why not go for a double-decker instead of a coach,' I thought to myself. It just so happened that a pal of mine, Sean Bentley, worked at the local bus garage. I nipped down to see him and arranged to rent a double-decker, complete with driver, who would be Sean. My next task was to turn out the biggest collection of Chelsea since the glory days of the Seventies and Eighties. If we could get to grips with Man U it might just be the biggest battle in the annals of football hooliganism.

Tony Covelle stayed with me the night before the game and we were up at seven, ready to head straight for The Star in Hampton Hill Street. I had arranged for the pub to be open at eight, with beer, sausage and bacon rolls for the lads. As they started to filter in I began to feel good about what was to come. More than 130 turned up and they were all top lads, good strong boys who would not give an inch, people you would want beside you in the trenches when the going got tough. There was Nightmare, Stuart Glass, Covelle of course, Muzza, Nathan Wharf, Paul Costa, Paul Lorda, Carney, Andy Cruickshank and many more. The only notable absentees were the twins, who, unfortunately, were in jail.

If that wasn't enough, we had an ace up our sleeves. Seventy of us had tickets for the Man United end of Wembley. By rights we shouldn't have been allowed within a hundred miles of their seats but thanks to 'our friends in the North' the tickets had found their way into our hands. The delivery driver had a huge batch to take to Old Trafford but, somehow, seventy of the precious briefs went walkabout and ended up in the hands of the Headhunters. How did we do it? That's a trade secret! It certainly wasn't cheap because we had to pay £250 each for a ticket. But that didn't bother us in the slightest. If we could get in among the Red Army we would cause fucking mayhem.

It would be one to tell our grandchildren about.

By quarter past ten it was time to leave the pub and get on our way. To ensure the mood on the bus was just right I had posters with the skull-and-crossbones (the symbol of the Headhunters) printed up and we stuck them up on the windows. We nicknamed it the Hate Bus so that no one watching as we passed would have any doubt about who we were and what we were up to. The maximum allowed on was 86 but when we did a head count there were 127 bodies. Luckily, the driver was my pal Sean and, just to be sure he stayed sweet, I promised him an extra drink when we got to Wembley.

The atmosphere on the bus was buzzing from the minute we left but it reached fever pitch as we went through the likes of Hounslow – which is mainly an Asian area – where the Chelsea songs got louder and louder and bottles were thrown out of the windows. By this time there was so much drink and drugs going about that the bus could have driven to Wembley on its own. A few minutes later and we were entering north London, Kilburn to be precise, where we treated the locals to a rousing rendition of 'No Surrender to the IRA'. To me Kilburn is Provo territory and it always has been.

We had arranged to meet the rest of the firm at the Lily Langtry on Kilburn High Road. The bus parked round the corner and we got off and moved as one to the pub. As we turned the corner onto the High Road, we saw about three hundred Chelsea outside the Langtry. Seeing such a herd of us so tightly packed, they thought from a distance we were Man United but then people start recognising each other and it's all shaking hands and 'how are you mate'. More drinking follows and by now we are ready for fucking anything.

A white Transit van passes. Three geezers are in the front, eyeballing us. Fuck me if I don't recognise one of them. He is none other than Alan Foskit, a Cockney Red and someone I had known my whole life. Although we are friendly, I know he is to here to spy on us and report back to his United pals, who are in the Black Lion at the other end of Kilburn High Road.

I waved and smiled at Alan. We are now desperate to get at them. The buzz you get in those moments is electrifying. But today was something else: the tension, the anticipation, the desire for it to kick off, and, inevitably, the fear. Only people involved in the scene will understand. These feelings are overwhelming and they spread like a virus through the pub and obviously we really wanted to win.

Six hundred faces. The biggest, and best, Chelsea mob I have ever seen. We march down the High Road, an invading army hunting the enemy, and get within twenty yards of the Black Lion. It's now or never.

Then we see them. Not the Red Army but a paramilitary force decked out in boiler suits, gas masks and riot shields. The Old Bill's timing is perfect, helped no doubt by the helicopter that is hovering above our heads. Five rows of Robocops appear from nowhere and block our path to the pub, willing and able to smash heads and break bones. The Old Bill, like us and United, were well up for it. They were very good that day.

Our disappointment is crushing. All the planning, all the bravado; all the pre-match talk about what we were going to do to the Red Army. All for nothing. There was one consolation. We still had our tickets for the United end and as the saying goes it ain't over till it's over. I successfully negotiated the first hurdle, the turnstiles, and began my ascent of the hundreds of steps to the section of stand my ticket was for. When I got there, slightly out of breath, I was confronted by a man with a happy, smiling face.

'Thanks for your ticket, Jason,' he grinned.

It was a Chelsea Old Bill. As he confiscated my precious brief he told me the whole batch had been reported stolen, before chucking me out of the stadium.

I jumped in a cab and sped off, back to the Lily Langtry, where many more of the gallant seventy were sitting, having also been thrown out of Wembley. What a fucking day. No agg, £250 down the drain and the Old Bill having a right laugh at our expense. I wondered to myself if things could get any worse.

Too right they could. Man U beat us four nil with Cantona playing a blinder.

Incidentally, I later found out how the Old Bill knew where we were going. One of our spotters told me that football-intelligence officers had someone not just outside my house but also outside the gaffs of Andy Frain and Tony Covelle. Our spotter also said we made the Old Bill's work easy for them because Tony stayed at mine that night and Nightmare went into the Star at eight in the morning. All the law had to do was follow the Hate Bus to Kilburn High Road, which took them to the heart of our little expedition.

14

Into Europe

The only good thing about our defeat to Man U in the 1994 FA Cup final was that it got us into Europe. They had won the title and would go into the Champions League, leaving us with the consolation prize of the European Cup Winners Cup. That's the way it was for Chelsea in those days, crumbs from a rich man's table, scraps of this and that. I didn't mind. It would be a great chance to go onto the Continent and show what we could do with my beloved Chelsea.

First up was Viktoria Zizkov from Czechoslovakia, who we had beaten 4–2 in the first leg at the Bridge. The away leg was meant to be played in Prague but at the last minute it was moved to the town of Jablonec nad Nisou, which is close to the border with Poland. Muzza, Andy Cruikshank and I got cab from Prague, which took about an hour. During the journey Andy was doing his best to talk to the driver but he didn't speak English. At this point Muzza butted in. 'I can speak a bit of German,' he assured us.

'Go on then Muzza. Have a go,' Andy said.

'How many kilometres? What is the costa?' Muzza asked.

The problem was he wasn't actually speaking German, but English with the worst German accent you have ever heard. Talk about the typical Englishman abroad. Andy and I were pissing ourselves.

In the end the taxi fare was only about £50, peanuts for us but probably a week's wages for the driver. It really was a cheap place for just about everything. In the pub I asked the barman how much the champagne was. It worked out about £3 a bottle so I said, 'Give me three bottles mate.' He thought he was ripping me off by charging as much as three quid but the last laugh was on him. The only one who got taken for a ride was Muzza, who paid a £100 bribe to get Mark Alleway out of jail. He complains to this day that Mark has never paid him back.

The whole trip was a right good laugh. The only downside was that we didn't see much FV, although it is not always about that. There were locals out looking for Chelsea – let's face it there ain't much else to do out there – but about all that happened was that one of them pulled a butterfly knife on us. We chased him down the road until he was well out of sight.

We had high expectations for the second round. Our opponents were Austria Vienna and we knew that Arsenal had recently gone there and had murders with them. In Vienna, the night before the game, there were about sixty Chelsea in an English-style pub called the George and Dragon. It was a very expensive city to drink in and so we had bought a boatload of Absolut vodka in the duty-free shop at the airport. They used those old clay jugs like the Vikings drank from and we kept refilling them with the vodka.

'What are you drinking?' the barman kept asking, puzzled that we were hardly ever up at the bar buying more beer.

'It's just water,' we replied.

He could see we were lagging.

'It must be very strong water.'

'Yeah,' I slurred. 'It's the strongest water I've ever had.'

And to this day it still is.

After several hours of drinking vodka, we were desperate for some entertainment. Luckily for us, Austria Vienna turned up and decided to put on a show. They flared the pub. So a few of us went outside to look for them but there was no one around. Still, they had shown up and given us notice they might be up for it. This could get really tasty.

The next day I had a shocking hangover. I felt like shit and was being sick all over the place and I wasn't the only one. I just wanted to get home to bed. It was one of those days you think will never end, you know the kind I mean. But we had a game to watch and an opposition mob we expected big things from.

After meeting up again at the George and Dragon we started walking to the ground, about three hundred of us, with every expectation that it was going to go off big time. We reached a huge park, which is just outside the stadium, from where we could see a big Ferris-type wheel (for you trivia bods it is the one that was used in the classic film *The Third Man*, which was shot in Vienna). Then, a few steps further on, we saw them.

A big firm, maybe two hundred of the cunts.

A bolt of electricity went through every one of us. We pulled out our tools, ready for action.

'This is it lads,' we said.

The walk turned into a jog as we got closer to our prey. Close up we could see what they were wearing and their body language. It wasn't Austria Vienna. It was another mob of Chelsea, who as it happens were also well up for it. What a fucking letdown.

We trooped into the stadium, completely deflated. Thirty of us had seats for their end but we were surrounded by pricks who didn't want to know (for want of a better word, scarfers) and Old Bill.

We later found out that it wasn't Austria Vienna that Arsenal had played, but Rapid Vienna, who carried a much better class of hooligan.

* * *

If the first two rounds had been something of an anticlimax the trip to Bruges for the quarter-final was to be one of the most memorable we had ever experienced. Not because we ran their mob – that would have been a piece of cake by comparison – but because we took on the full might of the Belgian Old Bill and more than held our own. It was their own fault. They clearly viewed football fans, scarfers and hooligans alike, as scum; scum who could be pushed around. I hope we taught them the importance of treating people with respect.

It seems that the phone lines had been buzzing between London and Bruges in the run-up to the game. The British football-intelligence unit was onto to its Belgian counterparts warning them that Chelsea were coming and that trouble was on the agenda. To add to the feeling of paranoia, there were hundreds of snide tickets going about, which the police no doubt thought would result in Chelsea getting into the home sections of the ground.

The Belgian police went right over the top. They were nicking everyone and anyone: scarfers, young kids, you name it. As long as you were English you were getting chored. I had flown into Brussels before making my way to Bruges, where I was enjoying a few beers with Muzza, Andy Cruickshank, Stuart Shooter and a few of the other lads. We also got nicked and were herded onto a van before being whisked off to this huge warehouse surrounded by crash barriers and with barbed wire on top. There must have been five hundred people in there. Admittedly, many of them were Headhunters but most were just ordinary fans. The Old Bill had been highly efficient, ruthless even. And that was their downfall.

The spark that lit the fire came when a 70-year-old man was dragged in and like the rest of us he was wearing plastic handcuffs. He wasn't a threat to anyone. It was heavy-handed policing of the worst kind. We hadn't come to Brussels with any grand plan but the sight of that old bloke in cuffs pushed us over the edge. Some of our lads had blades while others had lighters, so we started cutting and burning the plastic cuffs off. Then the chant of, 'We are the famous, the famous Chelsea,' went up.

The Old Bill, so arrogant and confident when they were pushing people around, looked shocked. They were big, burly, bearded, fierce-looking cunts but their bubble had well and truly burst. Now it was our turn. We attacked. They had batons and also a giant water cannon but it didn't matter one iota. We were so angry, so up for it, that we battered them. We picked up the crash barriers and either threw them at the cops or used them as battering rams. When they dropped their truncheons we picked them up and struck them on the head and body. Talk about a taste of your own medicine! I will never forget the sight of one of our lads going crazy in front of the water cannon; he was so far gone that even when things had calmed down he was still going mental and trying to attack the Old Bill.

Even better, we found a way out of our temporary prison. The warehouse had automatic shutters so Stuart Glass got to the other end of the building and pressed the button. The doors opened and about two hundred of our main firm ran outside. I shouted to the lads to split up, to make it harder for them to recapture us. It was every man for himself and what a buzz it gave us. I kid you not it was like something out of *The Great Escape*, although unlike Steve McQueen we didn't have motorbikes.

Some of the lads got caught almost straight away. Stuart Glass jumped into a river, hoping to escape, and he was wading across when the Old Bill reached the bank. They were screaming at him to get out but he wasn't having any of it. 'No, go get someone from the British embassy,' he was shouting at them, nearly up to his neck in water. It was a good try but it was back to the warehouse for Stuart.

As the game was almost over by this time I decided to go for a drink with Darren Crewe and Muzza. However, another pal, Scouse, couldn't wait for a drink and ran into the nearest pub and ordered a cab and a beer. When his taxi turned up so did the police, who accused him of escaping from the warehouse. Scouse denied it but his 'runner beans' were soaking so he got nicked and taken back. I was in the pub all night with Muzza and Darren and some of the other lads.

We had such a good night we ended up in a pub in Blankenburg. I spent a load of money that night but lucky for me all my £20 notes were snide. I wound up like John Wayne looking for me horse. As a matter of fact I got so drunk I missed our flight home the next day.

I didn't give a fuck. That was the sort of experience you live for. Going abroad with Chelsea, standing with your mates, refusing to give in, going toe to toe with the police. Then a few beers and a right 'tin bath' in the pub afterwards.

* * *

Things off the field seemed to get better the further the team got in the competition. Chelsea knocked out Austria Vienna and Bruge, which meant we found ourselves in the semi-final against Real Zaragoza. I flew to Spain with Flynny, MK, Colin Gault, Stewart Shooter and Andy Cruickshank.

First stop was the city centre, where we got hammered in a bar. Some of the locals probably didn't appreciate the English taking over their pub and they started rowing with a Chelsea scarfer. It doesn't take much in those situations so, when a punch was thrown, it kicked off big time. The fight spilled out into the street and I think it is fair to say that we proper gave it to them.

There was no more fun to be had with the locals so, well beered-up, we slipped into the stadium. The ground was a shit-hole and we made it even worse by ripping up the plastic seats to throw at the Spanish Old Bill, who were heavy-handed and used to having their own way. Once the seats were broken, lumps of concrete fell off as well and, no, we didn't need to be asked twice. We launched huge lumps of concrete at the cozzers, prompting them to charge us. There were a lot of charges, backwards and forwards, with them having the upper hand one minute and us the next. At one point we really ran them. They proper backed off, not wanting it, and I don't think they had ever experienced anything like it.

Inevitably, police reinforcements arrived and they steamed into us, this time with heavy batons. We got a right fucking hiding: we had run out of tools and they hadn't. But to be fair I think they enjoyed it as much as we did. I was black and blue, as were most of our lads, and we had learned that the Spanish Old Bill are far more interested in handing out a kicking than in arresting and charging you.

I've always said that the foreign Old Bill look the part: smoking, stubble on their chins, drinking half a lager on duty, growling, tooled up to the nines. Whereas our Old Bill look as if they've just finished their homework.

Milan

In those days – the days that we rarely qualified for Europe – if Chelsea ever had a promising pre-season friendly on the Continent we were right on it. They don't come much bigger than AC Milan so when, in the mid 1990s, a game was arranged I was out there like a shot. It was a chance to see the San Siro and it was also a chance to see Ruud Gullit playing for us against his old team. More than anything, it was a real opportunity to test ourselves against the famous Milan Ultras.

I flew straight into Milan from Stansted with Muzza and Colin Gault. We had plenty of time to kill and although I promised myself I wouldn't drink that pledge didn't last long. After meeting other Headhunters, including Tony Covelle, on the main strip in the city centre, I went on the piss after about two minutes. I didn't always go on the piss at football but when you are abroad it puts an extra spring in your step. I said to the rest of the lads, 'Let's go to the Prada shop and rob it.' No one disagreed and so we made for Prada. Quite a few of us were in the raiding party and as the staff can't watch everyone we helped ourselves to the very expensive merchandise. After taking our ill-gotten gains back to the hotel we went out drinking again, staying in the pub until it was time to go to the stadium.

By this time we were all lagging and when we get to the ground who do I see but Ross Fraser, who is something to do with a Chelsea fans' group. Fraser had been on the telly and on the radio criticising the Headhunters for being bad for the club's reputation. 'Fucking criticise the Headhunters, you cunt,' I thought. In a split-second I made a decision to attack him so I went up to a stall and bought a massive Chelsea flag.

After taking the flag off the stick I steam into him and as I am doing him I get attacked. I thought it was his mates come to help him. In fact it was plain-clothes Old Bill, one of whom hit me with his walkie-talkie. It was a savage blow to the head, although as I was lagging I didn't really feel it. But I was now covered in blood and, not content with that, I was arrested and taken to a room under the stadium. A phone call was made for someone to come and stitch my head and I was told to wait there by the cozzers, who then left the room.

'Fuck this,' I thought. 'I am not waiting around.'

Yes I would get my head seen to, but I would also miss the game and then no doubt get charged with assault. So I got up, sneaked out and headed for the stairs. It was a nightmare. There were endless stairs to climb and I was also paranoid about being covered in blood. I kept thinking that the Old Bill would re-arrest me because I was so easy to spot with all the claret on me. The plainclothes cozzers would recognise me but I wouldn't recognise them. Eventually, I found my mates and hid in with them for the rest of the game.

Funnily enough I have never seen or heard from Ross Fraser since that day. But the cunt owes me £120 for my Armani shirt!

15

The BBC and Taxpayers' Money

Life was pretty good in the late Nineties. Here I was, playing a bit of football, watching Chelsea, having a laugh with my pals. I also had a nice little business: tyres, vehicle recovery, that sort of thing. Life was sweet. Then, when I was least expecting it, I got hit with a fucking great sledge-hammer. To my way of thinking, the British Broadcasting Corporation, good old Auntie Beeb, the so-called pride of journalism, stitched me up good and proper.

The end result?

I was given a six-year sentence in one of Britain's hardest nicks for something I didn't do.

Most blokes will proclaim their innocence to anyone who will listen and I can well understand Joe Public being cynical. But, to me, I was set up by one of the most trusted organisations in the land for the sake of an entertaining television programme. After you read what happened to me I am sure you will hold up your hands and admit: 'Jason, that was a diabolical liberty.'

I am not trying to make out that I was some kind of angel. In this book, I have given many examples of my involvement in organised football violence. I am not trying to hide any of that. But you should only get convicted of things you are actually responsible for, not the things that society believes you should get done for.

How, and why, did the whole thing start? I am convinced it was because the BBC was feeling the heat: faced with competition from satellite and cable channels and desperate to justify the licence fee it came up with a new investigative series called *MacIntyre Undercover*. It was going to expose the conmen, the fraudsters, the thugs, by using covert surveillance techniques out of the FBI's playbook. False identities, hidden cameras, secret microphones, tempting inducements. You know the sort of thing.

All of that costs a fortune. The *Panorama* programme investigates things like nuclear weapons, terrorism and the Iraq war. At the time it took around £100,000 to make an episode of *Panorama*; expensive, but then it is the Corporation's flagship current-affairs show. Compare that to the £300,000 it spent making the programme on me for *MacIntyre Undercover*. Yes, they shelled out three times as much on following around a few football hooligans as they did on investigating whether Saddam Hussein had weapons of mass destruction. And it is your money, paid for from your licence fee.

Actually, I am not even sure the BBC were that bothered about getting a conviction. They knew that football-violence-related programmes are very watchable and sell well abroad too. They were clever in what they did because they would have earned colossal money from overseas sales. I quickly learnt that the documentary had also been shown in Germany, Holland, Italy, Sweden, Austria and Australia, to name but a few countries.

I haven't yet mentioned the unprofessional way the *MacIntyre* 'documentary' was put together. The BBC shot 344 hours of film, which was then edited down to just sixty minutes of 'highlights'. This, in my eyes, was designed with one aim in mind: to show me in the worst possible light. An even more reprehensible tactic was the Beeb's attempts at what, in my view, amounted to entrapment. Their reporters posed as major drug dealers. And that is just one example among many of them trying to impress me.

Many people have asked how Donal MacIntyre, the presenter, Paul Atkinson, his main lieutenant, and the bosses at the BBC decided to pick me. Part of it is down to the firm I ran with. The Headhunters are one of the most-feared mobs in the country and the BBC obviously wanted a firm of that calibre. I was a leading member and with the help of their informant, Darren Wells, they had a chance.

I am also sure that the Old Bill gave them a steer in the right direction. At the start of the programme they showed a number of photographs from police files of suspected hooligans. How did they get their hands on them? I am sure you can work that one out for yourself. Whatever happened to confidentiality?

Now that I am identified as a target they move in. Not just MacIntyre and Atkinson, but dozens of people straight from BBC central. They watch my home, they tail me; they follow me into the pub. They are doing the homework for MacIntyre, who, of course, got the cream and took all the credit. Their first hurdle is to get to know me without giving the game away. They do this by scamming a good friend of mine: Heather Smith. What they do to Heather shows the extreme lengths they are prepared to go to in order to get close to me. Heather worked as a barmaid in the Jenny Lind pub. MacIntyre and Atkinson began to visit the pub on regular basis and got to know her.

What they did to Heather was a fucking liberty. After grafting her for a few weeks, Atkinson took her out, wined and dined her, gave her the impression he wanted a relationship. But all he wanted was to get closer to me, so that we could become pals and go to games together. He told Heather a pack of lies about himself, for example that he had a fleet of vans and that he wanted to contact me to see if I would be interested in a contract to change the tyres. It would be worth £100,000. Obviously I would be interested. I had a tyre shop. It was my line of business. So I was always going to say yes.

The lengths the BBC went to, you would not believe. Members of their staff would link up with Atkinson, and occasionally MacIntyre, in the Jenny. They included geezers, I was later told, called Snapper and Mikey. Quite often Snapper and Mikey would have girlfriends with them, who, in reality, were also BBC employees. Their wages, plus expenses, must have added up to a tidy sum and all charged to you, the long-suffering licence-fee payer.

The next untruth was even worse. Atkinson told Heather he had a cocaine habit and that he imported drugs. It was all meant to get back to me, to make me think that he was a player, a face, a criminal. He then told Heather he couldn't read or write. Why? To give the impression he wasn't able to travel alone, making it more likely that I would invite him to come with us to games. Of course it never happened because I never invited them.

The pretence continued. They now have to convince me that they are Chelsea fans and that they want to get involved in the football-violence scene. So MacIntyre reads up on the club's history. Then he gets a Chelsea tattoo to make him look like a real hooligan. But the problem was that it had the club's new crest on it, something I spotted right away. In the documentary it looks as if I have been taken in by the tattoo but the editing was done to make it look that way. I wasn't fooled for a minute. At the same time he takes to dressing in designer clothes, because that's what all hooligans do, right? And he hires a succession of flash motors, because all underworld faces drive motors like that. I also kept bumping into Atkinson and MacIntyre at Stamford Bridge. That to me was strange, because I had been going to Chelsea my whole life and had never met them before.

By this time they had also been living next door to me. The BBC rented a flat in the same block as me in Chelsea Close, which is in Hampton Hill. They want to make out that MacIntyre and I are good friends, that he knew me well, that we hung out together, that he had a real insight into my so-called criminal behaviour. It was bollocks. He was never in my flat. Not once. That shows we were never friends. After all, if you've got a pal in the same block of flats you would almost certainly invite him round for a drink or a cup of tea. But it never happened. I never even spoke to him for three months despite the fact we had been neighbours for that length of time.

However, it did give MacIntyre the opportunity 'accidentally' to bump into me. This day I was coming out of my flat when I ran into him. He told me his exhaust had gone and did I know anyone who could fix it. Of course he knew that my mechanic could do it and that was why he was asking me. It was just another ploy to draw me in. Anyway I sent him off to my mate Scratcher, who did the job for him. Then, maybe a week later, I am in the pub with my mates. MacIntyre is there too and he sends me over a bottle of Budweiser. He waves over and later, when he is going to the toilet, he stops at our table and says, 'Thanks for sorting the exhaust with your pal.' Me being me I later send him a drink back. I believe he has now broken the ice with me.

The truth was that I never liked either Atkinson or MacIntyre and the thing I found most insulting about the film was the way it was cut to make it seem that MacIntyre was my best pal. In fact I only saw him about twenty-five times during the entire eighteen months of filming and I never even asked him his real name, simply because I wasn't interested. To me he was always Macca. I just never felt comfortable around either of them, but they were always willing spend money on drinks, match tickets, plane fares, whatever. I didn't have to like them and when you've got a couple of pricks hanging around who want to flash the cash you put up with them.

As for the 'celebrity' Donal MacIntyre I didn't find him either funny or charismatic. He didn't have much of a personality. In fact I've seen more life in a tramp's vest. I found him to be a smug cunt but I have to stress again that it was hard to get a handle on his personality as I didn't see him that much.

As all this play-acting was going on so too was the serious business of entrapment. I am afraid that in this country's legal system there is no concept of the agent provocateur. Organisations like the BBC can lie, cheat, entice you with all sorts of illegal activities and you are the one who is left to carry the can.

On 5 November 1998, Chelsea were playing a European Cup Winners Cup tie in Copenhagen. The BBC obviously thought there would be the possibility of filming me getting into trouble over there. So what do they do? They pay for round-trip tickets to Denmark, with Atkinson flying out on the same plane. The same thing happened at a West Ham–Chelsea game: they pay for my ticket and drive me there in their car after watching me play football. The pattern is repeated for Leicester away, only this time they pay for Andy Frain's ticket as well. It shows how desperate they were to get something incriminating on film.

The best, however, was yet to come.

After about six months they asked to meet me in a MacDonald's in Hanworth. Eventually, after a conversation, they asked me if I wanted to earn some very good money. They said they were very big in the importation of gear and would I be interested if they put a deal on the table. They had gear landing any minute, they said, and would I be interested in moving twenty kilos of cocaine.

I made it clear it wasn't my game. 'It ain't a bit of me,' I told them.

But both he and MacIntyre are very persistent. They offer me part of their cannabis business but I change the subject to my tyre shop. It must have baffled them. They had a picture in their minds of me as some kind of underworld figure, because away from football it's a known fact that I am very good pals with, for want of a better word, villains. So they hoped that by posing as major dealers it would be easier for me to accept them, while at the same time putting me in the frame for drug offences. Surprise, surprise – my refusal of the offer did not appear in the documentary.

I put it to you that for an organisation like the BBC to get involved in such blatant entrapment is a disgrace. Evidence gathered by this method would never be accepted in any other country in the world. But in England, even if the police or people working with them are shown to have acted improperly, you can still be convicted. I am just relieved that I knocked back every one of their drug offers and that my refusals were captured on camera. But I am afraid you never got to see that. Because it would be boring.

BBC – please sue me if I am lying.

16

Very Misleading

I was told by police informer Darren Wells that a *Macintyre Undercover* programme about football violence, featuring me, was to be broadcast on the BBC. He pretended to me that he had been changing light fittings in the BBC studios and had seen a trailer for the programme. At first I laughed it off. My initial response was 'Well what's that going to say – that I support Chelsea? Surely everyone knows that?' But then I had a horrible thought and so I asked him: 'I don't suppose it's got anything to do with those two flash mongrels I've been taking the piss out of, has it?'

Wells told me more about the programme and, as he did, it started to dawn on me what had happened. I went to a brief to try and get the programme pulled from the schedules or, failing that, to get an advance copy. But when you are up against an organisation as powerful as the BBC you have got no fucking chance. I was told the broadcast would go ahead as planned and I would not even be given the courtesy of a preview. So one night, in November of 1999, along with 7.4 million other viewers, I watched it, in the company of my brief.

It starts as it means to go on: with misleading and irrelevant bullshit. In the opening shots Macintyre is holding up a sheet of paper and his voiceover informs viewers that:

> This is a sheet from police files. It's a rogues' gallery of some of the most dangerous hooligans in the country and, what is more remarkable, they all follow one team. Collectively, they are known as the Chelsea Headhunters. The file reveals an intimidating record of violence.

What they have done is to plant a little seed in the minds of viewers. By using information provided by the police they now have official approval for the allegations that will follow. It means that anyone mentioned in the programme will be tarred with the brush of being a hooligan, whether or not they have actually done anything wrong. (It also shows that the Old Bill must have colluded with the BBC, despite their claims that they don't divulge confidential information.)

This is followed up by more misleading statements. According to the BBC and MacIntyre we are at the heart of an organisation whose organisation would put the mafia to shame. This is, the film tells viewers:

> A world dominated by a small group of hardcore thugs who organise violence through a sophisticated network . . . and who are always one step ahead of the police.

Have you ever heard such rubbish in all your life? Football violence is pot luck. It's a bunch of geezers who are up for it if anything happens but there's no planning behind it. As for the 'sophisticated network', yes, we do occasionally use mobile phones, but the Old Bill are well aware of that and know how to deal with it.

As for us 'hardcore thugs' being 'one step ahead of the police' let me tell you how it really works. The cozzers have spotters at every game. We know them and they know us and they are watching us all the time, aware of exactly where we are and what we are up to. Apart from anything else I was a season-ticket holder at Chelsea so I had to sit in the same seat for every game. The police could have put a camera on me for the whole ninety minutes if they had wanted to. So much for being one step ahead of them.

The programme then goes onto claim that 'a hardcore few spoil it for the majority of decent fans'. Of course at the same time it shows young fans in club strips being taken to grounds by their mums and dads. The implication is that the barmys (as we call the average supporters) are somehow in danger from hooligans. It's crap. We only fight our own kind. If someone hit a barmy they'd be called a cunt by the rest of the firm. No dad taking his kid has ever been in any danger because those who know the FV scene know one thing: you don't accidentally get caught up in trouble; you have to go looking for it.

After that build-up, the Beeb now needs something dramatic to keep viewers hooked. So the film shows scenes of violence from the 1998 World

Cup. We are told about the 'full riot' involving 'England hooligans' that started on a Friday night and went on for nearly three days. Fair enough. But I was never on the streets of Marseille at any point; I was at the England–Argentina game. The film was also edited to make it look as if English supporters were at the root of the trouble. So in one sequence they show our fans coming around a corner, not causing any problems, and then in the blink of an eye, it cuts to footage of Moroccans and Turks fighting. Misleading or what?

In a related scene Macintyre goes into a bar, where he finds a group of Chelsea:

> In the middle of them, holding court in a bright yellow jacket, I spot a Headhunter. I instantly recognise him from police files. He and his friends are casually snorting cocaine off the tables. It is clear his violence isn't being fuelled by alcohol alone. His name is [I have deleted his name], leading Headhunter and a friend of Jason Marriner.

Of course there is no footage of 'the leading Headhunter' being involved in any 'alcohol or cocaine-fuelled violence'. There is one simple reason for that: he didn't carry out any acts of violence. Let's face it, with a bright yellow jacket on he would have been pretty easy for the French Old Bill to spot! Why they decided to throw my name in I have no idea. I wasn't in the bar. It is another example of the BBC's piss-poor standards.

To be fair, however, there was concrete evidence of real football violence on English soil involving English clubs in the programme. Not even I can argue with that. Any straight member would have been horrified by what was unfolding on their screens. Pitch invasions, bottles and stones being thrown, lads being led away with blood pouring from their wounds, the police under pressure. It was the ugly side of English football and the BBC had no choice but to bring it into the open.

The problem was that it had nothing to do with either Chelsea or with me.

The footage was taken from inside a Manchester City–Millwall game. That's right, City versus Millwall. Most people watching the programme would have thought, however, that the violence was related to the Headhunters. Why? Because when they cut away from the trouble inside the ground to trouble taking place outside, the commentary used was from a Radio 5 Live phone-in about a Leicester–Chelsea game.

You've got it in one! The pictures were from Man City–Millwall, the soundtrack was from a phone-in about Leicester versus Chelsea.

It was a disgraceful piece of editing and, to me, it was done with a single overriding principle in mind: to blacken the name of one Jason Marriner. They were thinking: if we throw mud some of it will stick.

If you thought they couldn't pull any more strokes you would be wrong. In my view, the most misleading scene in the film is the infamous telephone-box 'intimidation'. I'll let MacIntyre give his account first:

> August, the first home game of the season for Chelsea. . . . Among the fans I get my first glimpse of Jason Marriner, harassing a man in a phone box. He's a committed Chelsea supporter and has a season ticket, but he's also committed to violence, which is just as important.

Actually, I was having a chat with the geezer and far from intimidating him we were having a laugh about the state of the birds decorating the phone box. At one point I have my arm outstretched, but that is not an aggressive gesture. In fact there is no violence shown in the clip, despite the completely false allegation that I am 'committed' to it. The film – which was edited down from several minutes to twenty seconds – also cuts out the part where I (very politely) hold the door open for the next user. Funny that.

The most detrimental part of the programme for Andy and I is the section on Leicester away. It is the game that gets us put away, no doubt about that. But conspiracy to cause affray? Violent disorder? In the film they couldn't come up with one act of violence from the Leicester game; neither in the footage that was broadcast, nor in the unseen material. Don't you think they would have been desperate to put something intimidating on screen? Chelsea fighting with Leicester would have been perfect, but they had nothing. Not a thing.

All they had was talk. Most of it intended as a wind-up.

Far from planning violence I didn't even know if I would be going to Leicester. The broadcast confirms that I wasn't sure about making the trip, probably the only time it got anything right.

> Jason Marriner: 'I don't know. I'm in so many different fucking minds, eh, I was gonna drive up and go on the Friday, see, now I haven't got a game on the Saturday and Sunday, I might fucking . . . I don't know what to do. You know, what I mean, cos I might have the light ale now.'

Donal MacIntyre: 'Yeah, yeah.'

Jason Marriner: 'I might have a drink.'

Donal MacIntyre: 'Well, that's the thing you know.'

Jason Marriner: 'We're meeting we're meeting early. We're meeting like Loughborough, probably Loughborough, which is one stop before Leicester, as we've got three coaches and a minibus going, it's naughty, Leicester will be naughty.'

Donal MacIntyre: 'Yeah.'

Jason Marriner: 'Leicester will be naughty.'

Donal MacIntyre voiceover: 'Naughty means Jason is planning trouble.'

No it doesn't mean that at all. I used that word on some of the unseen footage to describe a travellers' funeral I attended and there certainly wasn't any violence there. It was three hundred mourners having a laugh and getting drunk. In other words, being naughty.

As it happens me and Andy did go up to Leicester. MacIntyre gave me a lift and, as he explains in the film, there were another two passengers in his car:

> One of them is Andy Frain, the most dangerous of the Headhunters, and a man with strong links to both extreme loyalists and the far right .... Andy and Jason are helping co-ordinate 150 Chelsea hooligans as they travel up the M1 for a showdown with the Leicester fans.

Most of the details given in the film about that trip are bollocks. We were having a right wind-up; making daft phone calls to our mates, hardly able to a straight face most of the time. It was our way of livening up a pretty boring car journey.

Unfortunately, the wind-ups would later drop us right in it.

It was the infamous 'phone call' to Dalby (one of Leicester's main faces) that caused the most damage. But what I will never be able to get my head round is how me and Andy got found guilty on a conspiracy to commit violent disorder. To be guilty of conspiracy you first have to conspire. I am fully aware that a phone call was made but I am also fully aware that no one answered the call, let alone Dalby. Surely someone has to answer the call to make it a conspiracy.

To this day I would like to know how the jury found us guilty of a phone call that never got answered. I could go further and ask how the Crown Prosecution Service thought they had enough to charge us with what they did in the first place. But I suppose when they know they can get hand-picked, middle class, straight members on the jury the odds are always in favour of them getting a conviction.

The same distorted editing was used about a Chelsea away game against FC Copenhagen in the second round of the European Cup Winners' Cup in November 1998. We were in the pub, as was MacIntyre. Because Hickey's brother Sam was there, the conversation turned to the good old days of the Headhunters and how my old mate Hickey had got compensation after the notorious Operation Own Goal was found to have fabricated evidence, something that MacIntyre explained in his voiceover. Little did I know that history was about to repeat itself, because, to me, the way the next bit of footage is presented is probably even worse than what happened to Hickey.

> Donal MacIntyre voiceover: 'Jason is now in full flow and tells me other stories.'
>
> Jason Marriner: '. . . his brother, you read any football-violence book, anything like that, he is one of the most well-known football thugs you'll ever come across.'
>
> Donal MacIntyre voiceover: 'His stories are cut short only by his enthusiasm for the task at hand.'
>
> Jason Marriner: '. . . here we go; we've come to have a war.'
>
> Donal MacIntyre voiceover: 'I don't want a war but I can't say goodbye to Jason as we have tickets together for the game.'

You can clearly see the tape has been cut here. The brother I am talking about is still Hickey, Sam's brother. So, when I say 'we've come to have a war' it is me reporting to my listeners what *Hickey* once said. In fact it is him giving an inspirational speech to the lads before a Milk Cup semi-final against Sunderland in 1984 (which is covered earlier in this book). Hickey talks in a completely different way to anyone I have ever met and anyone who knows me will realise that I just don't speak that way.

But the BBC doesn't care. It wants to show that I was there to 'start a war' and editing the film that way makes me look bad. To make me look even worse they dub screaming sirens onto the soundtrack straight after I

(clockwise from top left)

Gate 13, east stand lower. Guaranteed to have fun in those days. I'm in the middle.

'I was there when we were shit.' That's me on the left – dodgy barnet and sta-press trousers.

Another away game, early Eighties. I'm in the blue jumper.

They reckon I could have a game when I was younger. A few of my hard-earned football trophies.

(clockwise from top left)

Jablonic. Me drinking a £3 bottle of shampoo. Hickey with a two-bob bottle of lager; **The man himself,** Ken Bates, in Jablonic; **My good pal** Darren Crewe in Rome. Left us too early. R.I.P.; **Real Zaragoza versus Chelsea,** 1995. Plenty of fun in the sun; **Bruges:** the great escape. I got out of my cuffs and the warehouse.

One of many pictures my good mate Charles Bronson has done for me.

(*clockwise from top left*)

Me and Super Ally McCoist at the shithouse (Parkhead) for an Old Firm game; **I love** everything about this club; **A poster** from my *Football Factory* road-show; **Working** for our beloved Queen at HMP Springhill.

Proud to call this man my friend. Freddie Foreman and me in Marbella, many years ago. (*above*) Me and another close pal, Howard Marks. He is a true gentleman. (*below*)

Sadly, Pretty Boy Shaw is not with us any more. He was a real friend, a top man. (*above*) With the legend that is Bruce Reynolds, the brains behind the Great Train Robbery. (*below*)

All in a day's work on ITV'S *This Morning* show.

Me and Carlton Leach on the piss in Puerto Banus.

After one of our shows together. Razor's nearly as funny as me!

One of many shows I did with my close pal,
Danny Dyer (*top left*)

My beautiful missus, Stephanie (*top right*)
Our little boy, Frankie (*bottom left*)

My other boy, Billy.

have spoken, to give the impression that trouble has broken out. But the sirens weren't Old Bill – they were on fire engines, something of course that is never explained.

In fact there was violence before and after the game with Copenhagen. The film makes that clear. But it also makes clear that it was Danish fans who instigated the trouble:

> Donal MacIntyre voiceover: 'Outside tension is mounting, as Danish start targeting Chelsea. I don't make it. I'm attacked by a Copenhagen fan. . . . I've just been beaten up, kicked, punched and thrown on the street by a bunch of Copenhagen fans.'

By the way I don't believe MacIntyre was beaten up by Danish lads. To me it was all staged by the BBC to make the programme sexier. But he did get one thing right. Copenhagen's firm were out looking for trouble that night, as I discovered to my cost when I was on the way to the boozer after the game. As I turned the corner I ran into twenty of the cunts and one of them threw a punch. I had a row with him but when more of their lads joined in I got punched and kicked all over the shop.

I only managed to escape by jumping into a cab and the driver, who was worried about the injuries I had sustained, insisted on taking me to hospital. There is an official record of the treatment I received from Amager hospital and it was produced at my trial. So much for me 'coming to have a war'.

Remember I mentioned my trip to Auschwitz with Andy? I explained it was a trip taken by almost every visitor to that part of Poland; it's for people who are interested in history and in particular the Second World War. But, surprise, surprise, that wasn't how they portrayed it in the film. This comment was also included as part of the Copenhagen sequence.

> Donal MacIntyre's voiceover: 'In a bar after the game he [Jason Marriner] describes a visit he and Andy Frain made to the Nazi concentration camp at Auschwitz.'

But it wasn't after the game. It was before it, something that the film itself proves because after the game I am clearly shown wearing a Hackett St George's Cross jumper, but, when I was talking about Auschwitz, I've still got my jacket on. In addition, the pub in which the Auschwitz conversation takes place is nearly empty and most pubs are full after a game. The BBC wanted to give the impression that my behaviour might incite a riot when all that really happened is that I was having a few cheeky beers with a couple of kids I knew before kickoff. We sat there, reminiscing about the old days, having a laugh, just like all football fans do.

The conversation, according to the film, went like this:

> Jason Marriner: 'They have a tour thing, right, and they're talking to all these Jerries about what happened, blah, blah. Frainy says 'take a photograph, Jase' there he is and the Jerries start going divvy.'
>
> Male anonymous: 'So you had a good week then?'
>
> Jason Marriner: 'Absolutely superb. I think I put the final nail in the coffin when I tried to get in the oven.'

As I have explained I went to Auschwitz because I am genuinely interested in history. But when I was telling the story in the boozer I wasn't giving the lads a history lesson. I was having a laugh. It was pub talk. I did take a picture of Andy. But as for getting in the oven don't you think I might have been joking? Apart from anything else the ovens are so small I couldn't possibly have got inside. I am a piss-taker and whether or not people think I cross the line with my humour is irrelevant, As far as I know having a laugh and a joke isn't a crime.

The Auschwitz part also gave the BBC the opportunity to wheel out Gerry Gable, the editor of *Searchlight*, the so-called anti-fascist magazine. Gable had already appeared in the programme, commenting on the (non-existent) links between the Headhunters and Combat 18. Now here he was again, talking about the Auschwitz trip:

> Gerry Gable: 'The group for the Chelsea Headhunters led by Frain paid a visit to Auschwitz concentration camp. I got a postcard from them, picture of the camp and on the back it said: "Combat 18 Headhunter division, wish you were here. We've just dug up the bones of your grandmother and pissed all over them."'

Highly offensive? Of course. Anti-Semitic? For sure. Pro-fascist. Definitely.

But there is no proof the postcard was ever sent.

If it does exist why the fuck didn't Gable show it to the cameras? And why didn't the BBC do what any reputable journalistic organisation would have done and ask him to produce it? I think you know the answer to that one.

Towards the end of the documentary comes the segment that would get me another two years in prison. Once again it is full of distortions and dodgy editing, all designed to put me in the frame. It was about the Bloody Sunday march in central London in January 1999, which is organised by Irish Republicans, many of whom make no bones about their support for the Provisional IRA. I was there all right but as part of a peaceful counter-demonstration against the IRA, something I am legally entitled to do in a free country.

Yet according to MacIntyre's voiceover I had gone there with violence in mind.

> I've arranged to meet Jason in a pub nearby, where he has already linked up with the leader of the Far Right faction, Combat 18. Jason's been planning to attack the march with them for months. I notice he's drinking mineral water.

This part of the programme starts with footage of a National Front counter-demonstration but that had nothing to do with me. The National Front were in Downing Street, I was in Trafalgar Square. I didn't want to stand with them because I'm not and never have been a member of any far-right organisation, whether it's the National Front or Combat 18 or whoever. And what's more no one has ever produced any evidence of me having such membership.

Apart from anything else it wasn't an event organised by the far-right, even if some of them were there. It was a counter-demonstration against the IRA, whose sympathisers were walking the streets of our capital city glorifying mayhem and murder. I was there as a Loyalist objecting to that presence, as is my democratic right. They tried to make out that the demonstrators were all hardened thugs who were out to make trouble. But let me tell you who else was there: members of our armed forces, one of whom had had his leg blown off. Doesn't the BBC think that he had every right to be there to protest against people who promote extreme violence?

The claim by MacIntyre that he had arranged to meet me is also false. I hadn't been on a march for years and even the day before I wasn't 100 per cent sure if I would go. The only thing that was definite is that, if I was going, I would meet Macintyre and Atkinson at Waterloo. As it happens I did go, with Andy, and when we got to Waterloo the two of them were waiting for us. It turned out that they had a grass keeping them informed so it was so easy for them to keep track of us. We know who that grass was, don't we?

The clever editing continued to make us look bad. This exchange, in the pub, makes it appear that I'm about to cause trouble.

Donal MacIntyre: 'What's this, mineral water?'
Jason Marriner: 'I don't give a fuck. That's ammunition mate. A bottle's a bottle to me. I don't give a fuck as long as it hits one of them.'

But Macintyre's speech was cut. He also said: 'It's Ballygowan water, that's Fenian water,' before I answered him.

Of course the BBC used it all to their advantage.

Donal McIntyre voiceover: 'As the marchers hand in a petition to Downing Street the extremists I am with are planning to pounce. Leading the attack is Andy Frain; in the front line is . . . Jason.'

The only thing they got right there was that we were at the front. The rest was bollocks. There was no bottle in my hand at that point and we later proved in court that no bottle was either thrown or broken that day. When we left the pub I was shown running, making out that I was going to attack the march but the reality was that we were late in leaving the pub and that was why we were running.

There is nothing in the film that shows us engaging in any violence or disorder. All they had was Andy and I running round a corner. That's it. The Old Bill didn't nick anyone on the day because nothing happened. I got an extra two years inside because I ran round a corner and shouted. A bit harsh don't you think?

As the programme comes to an end MacIntyre tries to sum up the last eighteen months in a voiceover.

There were many more moments that I recorded in my year as a hooligan. I went anywhere I thought the Headhunters might be. To Loyalist marches, to United marches for a fight that never happened, to Derby in the rain, even to Majorca when Jason failed to turn up. Jason continues to evade the police and has renewed his season ticket to Chelsea . . . Jason has taken me to the heart of the Headhunters and, after a year undercover, at last I was able to leave his world behind.

Let's unpick that statement.

Loyalist marches? We proved there was no trouble at the Bloody Sunday demo.

The Man U game? I went to it but, as he acknowledges, there wasn't any trouble.

Derby? I did go, but not with MacIntyre and Atkinson.

Majorca? As they admit, I didn't go despite them offering to pay for a whole week's holiday.

He also says I took him into 'the heart of the Headhunters' but if that's true what did he get? Nothing. Not one punch.

Like the rest of the documentary his conclusion was total bollocks.

17

No Daylight for a While

After the documentary went out everyone tried to reassure me. They said: 'You haven't done anything so you've got nothing to worry about, have you?' I wasn't so sure because it seemed that overnight I had become public-enemy-number-one. Don't believe the old saying that there's no such thing as bad publicity. That broadcast blackened my name big time and the first thing to suffer was my business, which went to the wall.

I went away for a couple of weeks, just to let the dust settle. After I got back nothing happened for a couple of months and I started to think I was in the clear. Well you would, wouldn't you? There was no evidence of anything illegal in the film despite all the BBC's distortions and lies. Surely a blind man could see that.

I got that one wrong.

Wednesday, 22 March 2000 is a day I'll never forget. Well, for starters Chelsea were playing Lazio in the Champions' League and I was looking forward to it. But first I had a business to run.

A kid called Aaron worked for me and I went round to his house at eight o' clock that morning to make sure he was up, dressed and ready to go. Sure enough he was in his car and ready to drive off when his mum came out and said Porky was on the blower. Porky ran an MOT station next to my tyre business and I couldn't work out why he would have phoned, knowing that he would see us in five minutes.

Then it dawned on me. The 'other' people were waiting for me.

As we approached my place, which was in Hanworth Road, I was keeping a serious eye out. Aaron drove into the yard and as he did so I noticed a typical Old Bill car opposite. It was unmarked but it stood out like a bacon sandwich at a Jewish wedding.

Porky came over to my car.

'Fucking hell mate. What have you done? They're everywhere.'

Then all hell broke loose. The 'other' people came from everywhere.

In my wing mirrors I could see two of the ugliest cunts I have ever had the misfortune to set eyes on. I hadn't spotted them before because they had been out of sight, hiding in their 'haddock'.

Don't ask me why because I couldn't tell you – maybe it was a rush of blood to the head – but in a split second I rammed my motor into reverse and swung out onto the main road. Laughing like a maniac I put my foot down, overtaking car after car. The Old Bill weren't about to let me get away with that. I understood that. But talk about 'on top'. I was chased by the Tactical Support Group, the Football Intelligence Unit and two 'undercover' cozzers in their Vauxhall. By the time I pulled over I worked out there must have been twenty-five of the cunts, just to arrest one man. And don't forget Andy was getting the same treatment, in Reading, so that was fifty Old Bill for just the two of us. Pathetic.

I had a quick look across the road and there were photographers and television crews everywhere. The Old Bill had leaked my arrest to the media, hoping for some cheap publicity. You would have thought I was a mass murderer to warrant that kind of attention.

One of the cozzers came up and said:

'Jason Marriner, I'm arresting you on conspiracy to cause violent disorder and affray.'

I laughed and when he tried to explain what it was all about I laughed even harder.

'Conspiracy, my bollocks. What are you talking about?'

One of the cozzers was obviously determined to put on a good show for the cameras. Desperate for his fifteen minutes of fame he forced my arm up my back, so I shouted, 'What are you doing you fucking prick?'

I was taken back to my yard in a big convoy and the cozzers ripped my tyre shop apart looking for anything incriminating. And do you know what they found? That's right, tyres. Oh, and my book of phone numbers, which was full of work contacts and friends, that sort of thing. I didn't know it then but they would use those numbers against me.

Eventually, I got taken to a nick in Staines and along the way I made a few sarcastic comments.

'I haven't been to Staines for a while but no doubt I'll make up for it with my length of stay today.'

'No you'll be bailed in a few hours,' one of the Old Bill replied.

I laughed. 'I've got as much chance of that as your old woman not letting the milkman in to tuck under her belt,' I replied.

The desk sergeant at Staines was a right funny cunt, or so he thought.

'So here he is then, the famous Jason Marriner. I bet you've got a police record,' he gloated.

'Yeah, I've got a few as it happens and my favourite is 'Walking on the Moon' but I always preferred The Jam,' I replied.

After I'd been searched I had to sit on a bench with two ugly plain-clothes gavvers. Then in comes this other geezer wearing a right dodgy Mr ByRite suit. His first words to me were, 'Do you know a Gregory?'

What the fuck was this cunt on? 'Do I know a Gregory?'

If a stranger came up to you on the Tube and asked a stupid question like that you'd think he was a right nutter. So I turned to the cozzer beside me and asked: 'Who's that geezer in the dodgy whistle?'

He started laughing. 'So you don't like his suit then?'

'No not much. Not only that. He wants to put some jam on his shoes and invite his trousers down for tea.'

That really set the cozzer off. He was pissing himself laughing but managed to blurt out, 'I can't wait to tell him that because he's our boss and he's the one leading the case.'

'Oh well that explains it. What chance has he got in life?' I said.

Probably more of a chance than Mr Funny Cunt desk sergeant who called me up for my details and asked if I wanted a solicitor. What kind of stupid question was that? Of course I wanted a solicitor. My brief was just waiting to find out what nick I had been taken to.

Chicken Neck – as Andy and I later nicknamed the officer in charge of our case – told us we would get bail. Once again, I just laughed. I knew there was no chance.

My brief arrived a few hours later so now it was interview time. Chicken Neck came out with all the reasons I was there and how he was going to play a video and ask me some questions. I read out a short statement, put together by me and my solicitor, denying any conspiracy to commit violent disorder and stating my rights not to answer any questions.

So that was it. Could I go home now?

Could I fuck. Just because I had the right to remain silent it didn't stop Chicken Neck from asking me endless questions. On and on he went, trying to get a reaction. But I just sat there staring at him and smiling every now and then. There was no fucking way I was going to make his job any easier. If you answer even a single question they will twist it and query why you didn't answer the previous questions, the implication being that you've got something to hide.

Later on that night, while I was in my 'peter', a gavver and two volunteers from the Friends of Prisoners came round to make sure I was being treated fair and square.

'Well I'm not getting treated at all because I ain't seen no cunt for hours,' I told them.

All I really wanted to know was the Chelsea–Lazio result and I said I would be really grateful if they could find out. They laughed as if to say, 'Is that all you're worried about?' However, ten minutes later, they came back and told me it had finished 1–1.

The next morning I was bundled off to West London magistrates' court in the sweat box, along with Andy. For those of you who don't know what a sweat box is it is a segregated box within the bus. In the summer it gets so hot you'd sweat your grandmother off, hence the name.

When I was in the court cell my solicitor, Huw Jones, came in to see me and we ran over a few things. Huw said that the BBC documentary had caught his eye as he had seen nothing illegal in it, nothing at all. I remember to this day him saying that it was the most overhyped documentary he'd ever come across, one with no substance to it. He went on:

'Jason, when I first saw the programme I was going to write to the BBC because I'd never seen so much shit in all my life. Why you got arrested is beyond me. We'll try and get you bail.'

He was the third person in two days to say that I might get bail. I knew he was clutching at straws. 'Come on son, there'll be no 'six-inch nail' for me today,' I told him.

I knew what the magistrates courts were like. Only 0.1 per cent of defendants get a not guilty. Not surprising when you are up in front of three beaks, one of whom is a churchgoer, another is the owner of a corner shop and the third a pillar of the local neighbourhood watch. Don't forget, they're doing this as a hobby and what kind of people do you think do it for fun?

They don't believe a single word you say. Yet they're happy to believe everything the copper says. Why's that? Because the copper is wearing a uniform and so he must be telling the truth, right? You and I both know that is crap. Just look at all the miscarriages of justice that have been uncovered in recent years. Football fans, not just casuals, are a convenient target for the authorities. They are easy to stitch up. Take Hillsborough, for example, where ninety-six innocent people got killed. As we are finding out, the Old Bill lied through their teeth about what happened there. It happens every day in our legal system.

The Crown Prosecution Service must have known there was no evidence in our case. So why did they take it so far? Because they knew with all the publicity it was high-profile and that juries are notoriously unsympathetic to those facing terrorism and football-violence charges. The defence is up against it from the start and you can forget 'innocent until proven guilty' – you're guilty in their eyes and somehow you've got to prove your innocence.

As I stood there in the dock next to Andy (not for the first time, I might add) my brief did make an application for bail. But like I said the whole system is rigged. And they were desperate to get the bail application thrown out, so desperate that they claimed I had given MacIntyre death threats. Now I admit that when I found out about the programme I did phone him up.

'I know about the programme, you dog. Are you happy with what you've done?' I asked him, at which point I put the phone down. But from that moment on there was no further contact. And why would I get in touch again? I wanted nothing more to do with him. If he did get death threats it had fuck all to do with me.

One really funny thing happened in that hearing. In fact it made me laugh out loud in the courtroom. The prosecution told the three Muppets on the bench that I had MacIntyre's name and address on a piece of paper in my pocket. Why the fuck would I have his name and address in my pocket when he had been living in the same block of flats as me, as a neighbour, for the last eighteen months? Of course, it goes without saying that the Old Bill couldn't produce the said piece of paper because they had lost it. What a coincidence! It was great police work considering I had only been arrested the day before.

When bail was refused I got taken to Wandsworth prison in the old sweat box. And then something else happened that made me laugh. On the way there, guess which song was playing on the radio? That's right, 'I'm an Innocent Man' by Billy Joel.

But what had just happened to me was no joke. I was about to spend the best part of ten months in one of Britain's hardest jails before facing trial.

For now I was Marriner FR 4629.

18

The Trial

Ten months in any jail is a long time but especially in Wanno, one of the sorest in Britain (of which more later). It meant that if my co-defendant, Andy Frain, and I had been found not guilty (as of course we should have been) it would have meant they had nicked nearly ten months of our lives. My strongest emotion, as the time passed, was to get the whole thing sorted as quickly as possible so I was actually relieved when, on 13 November 2000, the trial started.

That didn't mean I wanted it to be rushed and not run properly. But from day one Judge Byers, it seemed to me, was in a hurry. I'll give you one example. On the third day my QC pointed out that only two-thirds of the material that the prosecution had to make available had been made available to my defence team. How can I have a fair trial when the whole prosecution case is based on covert surveillance of me, some of which is now missing? But the little matter of missing evidence wasn't going to hold things up, as Byers ruled.

> The situation is different to police covert surveillance. The police have a duty not to edit. . . you can comment that this is less reliable [but] I conclude that, though regrettable, not all of the tapes have been served . . . I am also satisfied that the trial process is capable of dealing with the matter of gaps . . . on the big picture a fair trial is possible. It is incumbent on me to ensure that this is so.

It started badly. Then it went right downhill . . .

The next item discussed was quite unbelievable. It was an application from the prosecution to screen BBC witnesses from the public gallery because of concerns about their 'security'. Both Andy's QC and mine knew this would be incredibly prejudicial to our case and opposed the application. Even Byres had to agree and he threw it out. But when MacIntyre arrived in court escorted by two burly minders it must have had the same sort of effect on the jury: the 'brave' undercover journalist in fear of his life from 'out-and-out thugs'. The members of the jury must have thought there were two really dangerous men on trial if MacIntyre needed heavies to protect him. What happened to the presumption of innocence and the guarantee of a fair trial?

The only thing I had in my favour was my QC, Michael Wolkind. He was mustard and didn't miss a thing. Not only is he clever but also he is comical with it. We clicked right away and got quite pally. While other defendants might be talking about their cases during breaks in the proceedings we would be talking about football.

'Who've Chelsea got at the weekend?' he would ask.

'It don't matter. I'm not going, am I?' I would reply.

You might think my jokey answer showed that I wasn't taking the trial seriously. But the way I look at it is: the time to be serious is in the court room not when I am banged up in a cell or having a chat to my QC. You can't worry constantly about whether or not you are going to get a not guilty. I had confidence in Michael and I knew he would do his best for me.

I didn't think as much of Andy's QC but at least he did raise the issue of the shoddy journalism in the BBC's other *McIntyre Undercover* programmes. There were originally going to be six in the series. One was never made and we will never know why. Another, about insider dealing on the stock markets, was made but never broadcast. Another dealt with the world of modelling, in which it was alleged that young models were plied with drugs and encouraged to have sex with older men; it was later discredited. A fourth looked at a care home in Kent, which, after the inevitable public outcry, was closed after allegations of abuse against residents. However, a full police investigation found no evidence of systematic abuse and the official report on the case highlights the many distortions in the documentary, including the 'journalistic licence' and 'the distorted editing and dubbing', before concluding 'that the integrity of the BBC video and audio evidence is doubtful'. The Old Bill even put in a £50,000 claim to the BBC for the resources it had wasted on the whole sorry mess.

So that just leaves one other programme plus mine.

Even the jury-selection process went against me. My case was originally scheduled for the Old Bailey. But then it got switched to Blackfriars, which used to be Knightsbridge Crown Court. So now the jury is going to be made up of people from Putney, Kensington and Chelsea, places like that. They were all going to be upper class. They were wine-bar people not pub people. They were stuck in their own little world and wouldn't have a clue about how most people lived, let alone football supporters. To make matters worse nine of the twelve were women, who were much less likely to be sympathetic to so-called football hooligans than men. Of the male jurors one looked like an uphill gardener, while another gave the impression of being a retired schoolteacher. Call that fair?

The 'evidence' me against was in effect the *MacIntyre Undercover* programme, as broadcast, plus another forty-five minutes of BBC filming chosen by the prosecution to be as incriminating as possible. But there were 344 hours of footage, most of which was not seen by the jury. The only bits they got to see were the bits that had been edited to make us look bad.

Michael Wolkind brilliantly undermined their case right from the word go: 'Ladies and gentlemen of the jury, the prosecution is right: this case is about two dangerous, dangerous men. They are dangerous to society, to the general public, to anyone and everyone. And their names are Donal MacIntyre and Paul Atkinson.'

After reminding the jury about the Kent care home fiasco, Michael reminded the jury that the facts of the case were all important:

'Count the weapons – *none*. Count the episodes of violence – *none*. Count the confessions of violence – *none*.'

He was right. There wasn't a single example of violence in the film involving either me or Andy, something that the judge would admit at the end of the trial. Michael also ripped the BBC's credibility to shreds regarding the shoddy editing, which, to me, must have been deliberately designed to give the wrong impression. Remember that episode in the programme about me 'intimidating' the kid in the phone box? Well, a senior video consultant was called and he testified that less than a quarter of the available footage of that incident was used in the broadcast. We also played the unedited version in court and it showed clearly that I was just chatting to the kid. Further on in the proceedings another expert witness confirmed that a later scene, with me apparently roaring like a maniac, had been lifted from one sequence and placed in another, unrelated, sequence.

The BBC witnesses for the prosecution also had to admit that their employees had blatantly tried to entrap me by posing as drug dealers. This comes out clearly several times during cross-examination but I will give you just two examples from the official transcript of the trial. The first one went like this:

> QC: 'Early on you adopted the guise of a drug dealer, is that right, from the start of your meetings with Mr Marriner?'
> Donal MacIntyre: 'Yes, we did,'

And then a few questions later, this exchange was recorded:

> QC: 'Forgive me: prior to the Copenhagen pub, you were already in the guise of the flash drug dealers with the flash cars and the ready money, were you not?'
> Donal MacIntyre: 'Yes we were.'

The 1999 Bloody Sunday march, for which I had been charged with affray, was another blow to the prosecution's credibility. Michael asked MacIntyre on which tape could we hear Jason say he was going to attack the march. He couldn't answer that question and then he claimed that there had in fact been an attack. But the police admitted in court that no bottle had been thrown and that there had been no arrests at the march.

In fact the only reason I was charged with the affray was because there was film of me running round the corner towards the march. But MacIntyre was running with me at the time and Michael wasn't going to let that pass. He pointed out that if MacIntyre hadn't committed affray by running towards the march then I couldn't have committed it either.

When Atkinson was asked by Michael about the Bloody Sunday march the only thing he could say was that he thought I was going to cause trouble. It left their case in tatters, as this piece of cross-examination shows:

> QC: 'The 'bottle' conversation. Did you hear it?'
> Paul Atkinson: 'Yes.'
> QC: 'Did you realise the defendant was embarrassed?'
> Paul Atkinson: 'No. I believed he meant violence.'
> QC. 'Did you see him leave with it?'
> Paul Atkinson: 'No.'
> QC: 'Did you see him shout threats?'
> Paul Atkinson: 'No.'

QC: 'Did you see him throw the bottle?'

Paul Atkinson: 'No.'

QC: Is his 'plan of attack' on tape?'

Paul Atkinson: 'No. I wasn't recording.'

When the prosecution had finished presenting its case I took the stand and before my questioning started Michael gave a blinding introductory speech. 'In a beauty contest between Donal Macintyre and Jason Marriner, Jason Marriner comes second. He won't be on the front cover of the *Radio Times*. He was not invited to the BBC awards ceremony.'

In other words, don't judge a book by its cover.

I was in the dock answering questions for two-and-a-half days. I was never going to put on an act; I had made that clear to my legal team. My first words explained who I was and where I was coming from.

Let me tell you something. I come from the rough side of the road. I'm council, I've lived on a travellers' site for years, so don't you worry about my swearing because that's just the way I am. If I'm going to apologise to anyone for it I'll apologise to my mother or my father. I'm not an actor; this is me, full stop.

The best thing about taking the stand was that it gave me the chance to give my side of the story. I told them in my own words what a load of bollocks the programme was. During cross-examination the prosecution tried to make out I was one of the most notorious thugs in the country, which I said was laughable because I'd been filmed for eighteen months and I hadn't thrown so much as a punch. So what kind of thug does that make me?

Their answer showed just how desperate they were.

'No, Jason Marriner, that's because you are so clever you knew the cameras were on you, so you were the general of the generals and you got your foot-soldiers to do the fighting for you.'

'Well if I was that clever how come I didn't even know the kid living next door to me for eighteen months was an undercover reporter secretly filming me?' I replied.

Michael had done a great job of discrediting the prosecution's evidence and witnesses. Now we had a second opportunity to show what a load of bollocks they had been relying on. How MacIntyre had offered me drugs, not once but twice, in one of the most blatant examples of entrapment in legal history. How their insinuations that because I had friends like Hickey, Dave and Ian Sim and Tony Covelle proved nothing.

We also kicked the racist and far-right insinuations into touch. Roland Terry, a lovely geezer I'd known for years, took the stand. He is a well-respected man who managed a local youth team and we had known each other for about ten years. He is also black. After telling the court that I had helped him out with the team, for which I received no payment, he went on to say:

I saw Mr MacIntyre's programme and I do not think Jason was portrayed fairly at all. I have sat down with Jason over a pint down the years and we have discussed politics and race, among many other issues. Jason has made it clear when we have been discussing racial issues that he is not a racist and has said that, if he was, he would not socialise with black people or help me with the team.

I was shocked at the suggestion in Mr MacIntyre's programme that that Jason is involved with the likes of the National Front, Combat 18 and the British National Party and raised this with him. He told me that he is not a member of, or involved with, any of these groups. I would make the point that if I thought Jason was involved in this kind of thing and was a racist, I would have nothing to do with him. I would describe Jason as a friend. I think Mr MacIntyre has misrepresented his attitudes and behaviour. I have known Jason for a long time and the person I know was not the person featured on the programme.

You can't say fairer than that.

19

A Rapist Would Have Got Less

As the trial progressed me and Andy often discussed how it was going. Although we had been remanded in different nicks – he was in the Scrubs – we saw each other in the court cells almost every day. Having seen with his own eyes how weak the prosecution's case was he was pretty sure we would both walk out of there with a not guilty. Any rational person who sat through that farce would have come to the same conclusion.

It would all of course be up to the jury, and as I have already mentioned I wasn't that impressed by them. We had already proved that MacIntyre and Atkinson had offered me drugs, not once but twice, during the investigation. I had also told the jury that I worked hard to make a living and so being offered £100,000 to transport cars on my recovery trucks was huge. 'Could you earn £100,000 in a day?' I asked them. They didn't even blink and I knew there and then I was going to get a guilty.

Another thing I noticed was that there weren't enough notes being passed to the judge. That said to me that they weren't paying attention to what was going on. It was a bad sign. I wanted them to be writing away, taking notes; preparing discussion points for the judge or for later in the jury room. It seemed to me that they had already made up their minds and it didn't matter what we managed to prove. They didn't even seem to care what Roland Terry had said about me not being racist.

The problem was I had said things in the film that they didn't like, about the Leicester trip, about football violence. And after hearing that shit they just switched off for the rest of the trial.

It was on Friday, 8 December 2000 that the 'chocolate fudge' sent the jury out to consider its verdict. His summing-up took hours. You just couldn't shut him up but after what seemed like an age it was time. At half-eleven they trooped out, in front of a packed courtroom.

They say that if the jury is out for a long time you have a much better chance of getting a not guilty. They have more to discuss, to argue about, and that takes time. But the whole trial had been done in a hurry and I just knew they wouldn't let it spill over into the weekend.

Boomf, get it fucking done.

Sure enough, three-and-a-half hours later we were back in the court. It was a false alarm. They couldn't reach a unanimous decision. So the judge told them he would accept a majority verdict, if ten were of the same opinion. Another hour passed and we were back in court. This time it was the real thing.

Court official: 'Count one. Conspiracy to commit violent disorder at Leicester City versus Chelsea. Jason Marriner: guilty or not guilty?

Forewoman: 'Guilty' [majority: 11–1]

Court official: 'Count one, Andrew Frain: guilty or not guilty?'

Forewoman: 'Guilty' [11–1]

Court official: 'Count two. Affray at anti-Bloody Sunday demonstration. Jason Marriner: guilty or not guilty?'

Forewoman: 'Guilty' [10–2]

Court official: 'Count two. Andrew Frain: guilty or not guilty?'

Forewoman: 'Guilty' [10–2]

So that was it. Thanks to the BBC, the CPS, the Old Bill and a slack jury I was going to be put away for doing fuck all. Our briefs made a plea for mitigation but I had given up hope by that point. A ten was running through my mind, because to be truthful I had no faith left in the whole rotten system. The judge told the public gallery that if there was any disturbance he would clear the place. It didn't stop my mates from giving him a slow handclap though. It was gesture that I greatly appreciated, so thanks fellas.

As the judge read out my previous I saw that a couple of the jury members were nodding their heads, as if to say: 'We did the right thing. We knew all along that this man was guilty.'

Now it was time to discover my fate. I still can't believe what he said in his first two lines.

'Taking into account no evidence of actual violence . . .'

Yes, that's right. He really did say, 'Taking into account no evidence of actual violence . . .'

He was about to hand me six years in prison. So fuck knows what he would have handed down if I had been seen throwing a punch. Fifteen years? It was ludicrous.

He also said that I had shown no remorse for what I'd done. He was right about that. Because I had done nothing wrong.

Let's cut to the chase.

> I am firmly of the view that you are dangerous men, not just at football. You relish violence and will stop at nothing, with little regard for others or the law. You must be punished for what you have done. You will go to prison for a very long time: four years for conspiracy to cause violent disorder and two years consecutive for affray. That's a total of six years.

As he finished speaking I just thought: 'so fucking what'. I turned and looked at the jury, smiled and winked, and said to myself: you take that to your poxy wine bar and I'll take it to my grave. They looked at me with complete disgust as if to say: 'he can't stand there and smile at us'. But oh yes I could and I had every right after what they had done to me. Despite everything that had happened I still believed that good will follow bad, because even the darkest hour of your life lasts for only sixty minutes.

On top of my sentence the judge tried to impose a twenty-year ban from attending football. So here we had a High Court judge in charge of a very high-profile case who didn't even know the law. The maximum ban allowed by Parliament is ten years so he had to bin his original decision and make it a ten-year ban. And you wonder why I have no faith in the system.

The BBC of course took full credit for getting us convicted. On their website on 8 December 2000, director general Mark Thompson, referring to our trial, boasted that 'this outcome is a testament to the integrity and validity of the *MacIntyre Undercover* programme on hooliganism.' What a load of bollocks. It was sloppy and misleading rubbish from start to finish, as I hope I have shown. Never ones to miss an opportunity, the BBC also announced that a specially updated version of the programme was to be shown just three days later, on 11 December. Obviously, they didn't have much doubt about a guilty verdict being handed down.

20

Always Vacancies at Sunny Wanno

It was pitch black when we got led away from court. A typical cold Friday night in December. Fucking freezing. In the van Andy and I had been put in different sweat boxes because I was going back to Wandsworth and him to Wormwood Scrubs. I shook his hand and gave him a hug.

'See you later, son, stay in touch.'

'Yeah, sweet,' Andy replied.

They handcuffed me and the van drove off. All I wanted to do was get back to my cell, read the papers and get my head down. I had already done a big lump of my sentence and, although there was still a lump to do, I now knew what was in front of me.

I was sitting in my sweat box as it went to other courts to pick people up and I could hear all the stories coming out about how this one and that one had been stitched up. Then it came on the news.

'The two notorious Headhunters, Jason Marriner and Andy Frain, have got six and seven years respectively.'

'Fucking hell, that's a liberty,' someone in the van said.

I burst out laughing because he didn't know I was on board. Then every time we passed Curry's or Dixon's there I was on the six o' clock news, my face larger than life on the telly.

The difference was that my remand was over. I was now a long-term prisoner. But even though I had been there for almost a year I still had to see a doctor. He said he wanted to put me in the hospital wing for the night, because the sentence was probably a lot for me to take in. I told him in no uncertain terms I wasn't going down that road.

'If you think I'm going to hang myself over some judge giving me six years you're off key. I've got plenty going for me outside, thank you very much. Six years won't alter my life.'

So I signed a form to say I'd refused to go on the hospital wing and made my way back to my own wing.

Wanno is a sore nick, a horrible old Victorian dump that should have been pulled down years ago. You're banged up almost 24/7, apart from getting out for your three meals a day. I've seen grown men buckle in there it's that tough. In those days it was the only jail still run by the Prison Officers Association and that's why it was so far behind the times. The screws didn't want it to move forward because, let's face it, when you're banged up they don't have to work. It was so bad that some prisoners actually preferred seg. As my mate Dave – an escapee – told the governor before he was sent down the block:

'I'll get a phone call, a cell clean, a shower, and exercise every day and that's four more things than I'd be getting on the landing.'

If Wanno had a silver lining it was, strangely enough, the amount of time you spent in your cell. In the prison system Wandsworth is known as a bird killer because you know your daily routine and so once you've had your meals and you're banged up again it's another day done.

But I always say no matter which nick you are in, and how tough it is, doing time all comes down to your frame of mind. If you can stay positive all you care about is chipping away at your sentence. You get up and have your breakfast, then go back and do a little bit of this and some of that and before you know it lunch is being served. You follow the same routine in the afternoon and after tea. If you're lucky enough to have a radio, you might hear your favourite song or listen to a game. There's football on almost every day now and that is a massive help because when the full-time whistle goes that is another day done.

One thing you have to master quickly is how to deal with the kangas. You have to know how to work them because most of them have been doing the job for a long time and whatever else you might think of them they ain't fools. You're in Wandsworth, one of the hardest nicks, so you've got to graft them and get them on your side. And some of them weren't so bad, like this old screw, Mr Stewart, although his good points weren't immediately obvious.

I remember the first words he spoke to me.

'Canteen, cunt.'

Then when I got to the canteen he was still at my shoulder.

'Were you ready when I opened the door?' he asked.

'Of course I was. You saw I was already on my feet, didn't you?'

'Good,' he said. 'Because if you hadn't been ready, I'd have slammed the door shut on you and you wouldn't have had canteen for another week.'

I just looked at him.

'What? Do you really think I'm that bothered about getting hold of some poxy tuna and noodles?'

He thought he had got me.

'Oh, you'd have been bothered all right because you wouldn't have been able to buy fags.'

I batted it right back to him.

'I don't smoke.'

Give him his due, he was straight back in.

'But you must buy fags like everyone else, even if it's just to serve them up to someone later for extra phone card.'

'No, I've got plenty of other tricks for that.'

I had given him an answer for everything he had thrown at me. He liked that. He respected it. He enjoyed the cut and thrust.

I will never forget the sight of Mr Stewart on Christmas Eve when he came in lagging drunk with this big nose stuck on his face, wearing joke dreadlocks. He marched up to my cell door.

'Marriner,' he shouted.

Instead of jumping out of my skin I turned slowly to face him, as I was reading my paper. I was as casual as you like.

'What is it guv?'

'You're a cunt,' he screamed.

And with that he slammed the peephole shut.

Listen, prison is all mind games and he loved to play them. I've seen people fuming about him and I had to tell them, 'No he loves all that, but he's sweet. He's all right. Just play along with it.' I never let him get under my skin.

I remember one time he came up to me.

'Marriner, have you got any phone cards?'

I thought I'd have a bit of a joke with him.

'What do you want one for? Can't you use the public phone? No guv, I haven't got one.'

And with that he gave me one of his phone cards. Just like that. I'm telling you, he was all right for a screw.

Don't get me wrong there were some screws I fucking hated. There was this one kanga I thought was okay until this day he showed his true colours.

I was working on the hotplate, chatting away to two of my mates. Nearby there was this Geordie screw, a senior officer, but a right pisshead too. As we were talking this kid, a smackhead, walked past and said to the screw.

'Guvnor, I'm not being funny, but I've had three nights on the trot where I can't sleep because of savage toothache.'

The kanga wasn't interested.

'You can't sleep because you're on the gear again and you're clucking,' he said dismissively.

The kid might have been lying but at the end of the day the screws are there to provide a service and look after your wellbeing. But none of that mattered to this cunt.

The kid was still standing there, complaining about his toothache. And he went on and on until the kanga snapped.

'Fuck off. Who are you fucking talking to?' he bawled.

'You can't talk to me like that,' the kid said.

'I can do what I want. Now fuck off before I smack you in the mouth and then you'll have no tooth.'

I could see it was never going to end there and the moment the kid said something else – crack! The screw chinned him and the tray went flying.

Another kanga saw this and he blew his whistle. The kid got nicked and put on a charge. Now he was down the karaoke while the screw got away scot-free. But then they never go over on their own, do they? From then on I saw that screw in a different light. He was a bully who used his position of authority to take liberties.

Another important factor inside is keeping busy and one of the best ways of keeping busy is to get a job. There are also the little extras that come your way when you are working. Even when I was on remand I wanted to get one. You might have the best pad-mate in the world but you're bound to get on each other's nerves over a twenty-three-hour bang up. Try being in the same room as your wife for that long, seven days a week – and you can fuck your wife!

It wasn't easy to get a job. You had to apply for one and most of the forms ended up in the bin. It's another thing the screws do to test you. With them everything is always 'tomorrow' or 'wait and see'. One thing that might have worked in my favour was that I hadn't given them a lot of grief, not like those short-tempered kids who were always going up to them and shouting: 'You're a fucking prick.' If you are a character and give them the old yes-sir-no-sir-three-bags-full-sir routine they might even get to like you. Some people might think I am a cunt for doing that but it makes life easier all round. In that vile gaff that's what it's all about.

It also helps if you're not on the 'Chinese rugs' because the kangas realise you're not going to be interested in contraband and serving up. As the job I wanted was on the hotplate – where I would come into contact with the whole wing – that was important to them. So after three or four months on remand I got onto the hotplate and the day after I was sentenced I was straight back on it.

I enjoyed the hotplate, the banter with the lads, the fact that I wouldn't be stuck in my cell thinking about my sentence and all that had gone on. It also guaranteed you a shower and a daily phone call, plus you could clean your cell every day and wash the floor. Little things on the outside, but gold dust inside. And like any other job there were plenty of other bonuses: you could nick trays of chickens to razor-blade and also get your hands on those little reflective sheets we used as mirrors. That enabled me to look after my mates. Inside proper people don't forget.

There were endless opportunities for barter. I remember this big black American geezer who was in for fraud. I used to dish him up two extra portions of rice a day and at the end of the week he'd give me a half ounce of tobacco, which I would trade for phone cards or chocolate. It helped to make life more bearable.

The other thing that makes life worth living is support from people on the outside. I got plenty of letters and while it was great to get them nothing could beat a visit from family and friends. If you got a good visit – and I made sure all mine were good ones – you went back to the wing with a spring in your step.

I could always feel eyes on me in the visiting hall, the sideways glance that said, 'Do you know who that is? It's Jason Marriner, the one from the MacIntyre programme.' I didn't mind because it gave me a chance to show other people's visitors that I was human, despite what they had seen on the telly. The problem was that I couldn't pass up the chance for a piss-take. If a geezer had a female visitor I would go up to them and ask:

'Is that your lovely lady?'

'Yeah, this is her,' the geezer would reply.

'That's funny,' I would say, 'because the picture of the bird you've got on your cell wall doesn't look like her. She's got ginger hair. That's not the same bird at all.'

You could see the jaws dropping and the kid would be pleading his innocence as his bird didn't know it was a wind-up.

'Oh, drop me out Jase,' my mate would say.

I'm not that cruel so I would always tell her, 'No, I'm only joking sweetheart,' before walking off laughing.

As I said support from the outside is so important. So I was touched by the generosity of the lads I had got to know through football. I got so many letters and quite a few times they sent me and Andy a couple of hundred quid, and, let me tell you, when you're on £15 a week in the nick that makes you a rich man. As well as many visits from friends in the south one mate, Peter McBeath, came all the way down from Newcastle to see me. It's a long way and what made it even harder was that he had to get there by half-eleven in the morning.

But if we're talking about long-distances no one can touch my old mucker. Yes I'm talking about Hickey, Steve Hickmott, who, of course, got ten years after Operation Own Goal but when the Court of Appeal threw out his conviction he ended up with £96,000 in compensation. At the time he was living in the Philippines but he flew all the way over just to see me. He was wearing the same old combat jacket and jeans and I soon discovered he was as funny as ever.

'Why didn't you spend your compensation on some better gear?' I asked him.

'Because I would rather spend it on whores with sores.' he replied.

He went on. 'I've just flown six thousand miles to see you. Don't they know me? Do they really not know who I am? I've just had to wait outside in a queue.'

'What do you want? Special treatment?'

'Yes! I deserve special treatment. I've had enough of these piss-holes myself. Anyway how are you Jason?'

21

Time Stops for No Man

After about a year in Wanno the screws could see that I had played the game and was ready for a move to a C-cat nick. So I got sent to Elmley in Kent, which I was told was a twenty-three-hour bang-up. But, when I got there, about half-six in the evening, people were playing table tennis or on the phone or just hanging about. In fact, bang-up was at quarter to eight. Not only that, there was hot water on tap, which meant I could make Pot Noodle or whatever. The food was also much better: there were proper chips and proper portions and there was even a menu. Fucking unbelievable!

My only problem in Elmley was my high-profile status. I had eventually been able to get my dream job, as gym orderly, which meant I could train during my free time. Thanks to all the exercise I lost about two stones. I looked good and I felt good.

Then, just when everything was going well, I got swagged off the gym job by the head of security. Security runs prisons and has the final say. The gym senior officer told me he was gutted for me, and had tried to fight my corner, but I knew there was nothing he could do if his bosses had made up their minds. It was a liberty because the head of security didn't even know me. He was judging me by what he had heard and he even told me to my face that it was because of my high profile.

Later in my sentence my profile also stopped me getting transferred to Blantyre House, which is a D-Cat prison (by comparison Wandsworth was a B-Cat). I put in a request but was told they'd changed the criteria so that no one convicted of football violence could go there. It wasn't funny but you've just got to keep laughing at them. One screw asked me:

'Why are you so happy all the time, Marriner?'

'Well, why not guv?' I told him. 'I'm living, I'm breathing, I'm healthy,

122

I'm sweet and I'll get out eventually, unlike you. What do you want me to do: walk around feeling miserable every day?'

Even if they won't admit it to your face that is exactly how most of them want you to be, but they were never going to see me like that. I'll tell you something else about prison: you always have the last laugh even if you're doing life. When you pack up your gear on that final morning, and walk through those gates, always hold your head up because that is you having the last laugh. However much it gets up their noses there is nothing they can do, so make sure you enjoy the moment.

After nine months at Elmley I went for my D-Cat again. And this time I got it. I was off to Standford Hill, which, although it was literally across the road, was a million miles away in terms of how you were treated. The kangas' attitude was very much, 'If you want to fuck off, then fuck off, because no one's going to come looking for you. That's the Old Bill's job, not ours.'

Even when I came out of reception all I was given were directions to the wing and there weren't even any screws to escort me. What made it even better was that I got a single cell for the first time since I'd been number one on the hotplate at Wanno. But even though I was now in a D-Cat it didn't stop the knockbacks. I tried to get into Latchmere House, an open prison and resettlement unit, but again I was rejected because of my high profile.

When I went to my next nick, Springhill, near Aylesbury, it was an uphill battle to get the privileges I had earned by right. I had already been on a number of town visits from Standford Hill but when I went to the Risk Assessment Board about a possible home visit I got turned down because the World Cup finals in Japan and South Korea were on. Fuck me! I've done a bit of travelling in my time but to go the Far East, watch a game, have a fight and fly back home, all within an eight-hour licence. What's more, I didn't even have a passport; the cozzers had it. That's prison logic for you.

Having said that Springhill was a blinding nick. There were twenty-four to a hut, all in double cells. You had running hot water, your own sink and showers and at the end of each hut there was a television room. The other people in there were the best I'd ever met in the nick, real good lads most of them and we had so many great laughs. There were the likes of Lenny Hagland, Jay Usher, Dean Lingham, Simon Brown, Lol Ahearn and Billy Whiteley.

However, my battles with the system were fuck all compared to the one I had been fighting since the day and hour I was sent down. I am talking about my appeal, which was, as required by law, lodged within twenty-eight days of me being sentenced. Believe me you never give up from that day on and I bombarded my briefs with information I felt would be important in the appeal. It was partly because of the length of time it took to get a hearing in the Court of Criminal Appeal. To me the powers-that-be took the piss, stringing the whole thing out for as long as possible, using excuses like files were missing.

For once I got a stroke of good luck. A mate of a mate of mine had been on jury service at Blackfriars during the time my case was running and he met one of the jurors from my trial in the smoking room. It turned out the juror concerned had done corporate work for Chelsea. When this information reached me, through another mate, I immediately passed it on to my solicitor, Huw Jones, who in turn told Michael Wolkind. I immediately realised that despite the other important points regarding entrapment that would be raised at the appeal this new factor would be the key to me getting a result.

My mate Muzza was also a big help. He was at the 2002 FA Cup final, in Cardiff, and afterwards, when he was in the corporate suite drowning his sorrows, he spotted someone he half recognised. The penny dropped. It was the juror from my trial, the one who had done corporate work at Chelsea. Muzza knew that part of my appeal was to do with a juror so he went up and said, 'You look like so and so off the telly. Can I get my photo taken with you?'

The juror agreed and then Muzza, knowing that this could be important to my case, found out a very interesting fact from another bird he got chatting to at the hotel: the juror was a senior manager in the company that supplied services to the club, not just an employee.

One day, about three months after the cup final, I got a letter from Muzza. It read: 'Dear J. Don't get your hopes up, but I saw this bird at the Chelsea–Arsenal game.' Then I saw the photos of him with the juror. My reaction?

'Blinding. Get in there.'

I got on the phone to Muzza, to half-jokingly give him some grief about holding onto the pictures for so long. But that's typical of him. He's just so laid-back. But I was laughing because I knew he'd come up trumps for me. We still laugh about it now: I tell him he could have got me out three months earlier but he tells me he hung onto the photos to give me extra time to lose some more weight.

As soon as I came off the phone I was onto my briefs, who were able to confirm that the juror did work for a company connected to the club. Eventually, we got to court for my appeal, where Michael was his usual brilliant self. It came out that the juror in question had been involved in providing corporate services on nine occasions at Stamford Bridge, which meant that person should never have been on my jury. During my original trial the court was given the impression that it was only two or three times.

I should have walked there and then but the appeal was referred for judgement and I was sent back to the nick. After about four weeks I got a phone call from Michael telling me I had got two years knocked off and I could go home right away. I didn't know what to say so I just said: 'All right Michael. Thank you very much.'

The way I looked at it was I'd done my bird. I had served two years ten months and was only six weeks from my parole date. So despite the two years being knocked off I had actually done a six, not a four. That's because if I'd got the four at the original trial I would have been eligible for parole after two years. So I spent eight months longer in prison than I should have done. And what do they do? Give me back less than two months. I've spent longer in the canteen queue.

I had lost three years of my life in prison for, let's face it, doing fuck all. Even if I had been guilty of something it was still an excessive sentence. In Wandsworth I heard about a rapist who held a girl captive for two days while he abused her; he got a seven, only a year more than me, or six months if you count parole. I could give you dozens of examples like that.

So that was me back on the outside. Obviously a lot of people knew what had happened to me and they kept asking: 'Haven't you changed because of all this?' How was I meant to change? Was I meant to fall apart? Should I have let it destroy me? Am I going to stop being a character, the life and soul of the party? No; of course not. I was set up and I got a six stretch and I will never change what I am because of what was done to me. Anyway I can't turn the clock back. It's a lesson I learnt in prison: deal with the things you can do something about. You have to look forward, not back.

Get on with your life.

22

The Ultras

After coming out of jail in 2003 I kept a low profile when it came to FV. It was forced upon me to a large extent because I was banned from Stamford Bridge. But I still kept in touch with the lads, especially when we had a tasty one coming up. The Champions League round-of-sixteen tie with Roma was certainly in that category. Their Ultras had a big reputation and we had heard they were coming to London in big numbers, ready to put one over on us.

Our information was spot on. We were told that a big mob of them had been drinking in the West End all afternoon, bigging themselves up and mouthing off. I drove to Chelsea, getting there about five in the afternoon, where I met up with Martin King and Bully. We had a walk about and we got that old familiar tingle: something was going to happen, the only questions being where and when. We did have a problem though. Many of our main faces had been banned under the new system for dealing with football hooliganism, which meant they were not allowed within so many miles of the stadium and in fact were not even allowed to set foot in the town, city, district or borough where a designated fixture was taking place. My ban, which was under the old system, was different, and only prevented me from entering stadiums.

After visiting a variety of pubs and getting phone calls, a call came through to say that Roma were milling around outside the ground, striding around as if they owned the place, intimidating scarfers, generally taking liberties. That would never have happened in years gone by, when our full mob was on manoeuvres and Chelsea was such an intimidating place to go. It gave me the hump, because I didn't want the Ultras going back to Italy and telling everyone Chelsea weren't all they were cracked up to be.

Our next stop was the Elk, a new – and to me, poncey, pub – that I had never been in due to prison. I would say there were around a hundred of our lads in there, having a laugh and a drink. To me however it was far from a humorous situation: I kept getting calls, telling me that the Roma Ultras were here. After a while I said to the lads: 'Do you want them to go back and tell the Eyeties we're a bunch of cunts?'

I could see from their body language that they agreed but there were pints to be sunk, jokes to be told and old times to be recalled. But I knew they had taken what I had said on board and, with the seed sown, I left it at that for the time being.

Then, with about half an hour to kickoff, I made my second pitch.

'Half of our lot are banned and they ain't here. If they were here we would have done something about it by now.'

That had stirred them into action and so I asked: 'Who's going over to Roma?'

Most of the lads said they would go and I told them, 'I am banned and can't go. But let's get out of the pub and get into them.'

Everyone was up for it, but a couple of them wanted to finish their pint.

'Come on. Let's get out there and into these. When you go over there they will throw things, they will spit at you; they will try to intimidate you. Let's get out there and intimidate these cunts.'

My little speech worked. Martin King said, 'Fair play. I'll make you right mate.'

I managed to get everyone out of the pub and we marched straight to the ground. On the way we spotted a little mob of Italians. I had the hump. When we were right in the middle of them I smashed my elbow right in the face of one of the Ultras. Seeing what I had done, Bully said, 'Fucking fair play to you Jase.'

'That's only the start of it. It's only what those dogs will do to us over there.'

As we got closer to the stadium we saw two coach-loads of Roma getting off. They were trying to follow what they thought was the English habit of wearing Burberry scarves and hats but they were only ten years behind the times in the fashion stakes. They had sunglasses on their silly gel-backed hair. What's all that about? One, it's England, and two, it's a night game, so you don't wear fucking sunglasses.

Our pace increases to a canter and we let them know exactly who we are. That canter goes up a notch or two until it is a fucking sprint and we steam right in, punching and kicking and butting.

We took them completely by surprise. One minute they are standing there smoking, laughing and joking. The next minute we scatter them like ashes in the wind. It is our patch and they had been taking the piss, striding around our forecourt like they owned the place. Now they would have to take that home with them, with a few cuts and bruises for their troubles.

To me it's what Champions League nights are all about: testing yourself against the best, both on and off the field. We had looked good that night, walking down the Fulham Road to confront Roma. Maybe the old days would come back; maybe there would be more days and nights like this. Little did I know that the most momentous day of my life was less than twelve months away.

23

My Love for the Gers

The media have tried to hang the extremist label on the Headhunters, claiming that we are members or supporters of the National Front, the British National Party and Combat 18 and any other right-wing organisation they can think of. I have never been in any of them. Nor am I a member of the English Defence League. I defy anyone to produce a membership card or documents linking me to any of them. The media make up this rubbish in order to make people more anti-football-violence. It is also a myth that the Headhunters are racist. There were black blokes in the firm, maybe not that many, but it shows that we were open to all races.

What mattered to us was whether you could fight, whether you would stand with your mates in a tight corner. Not the colour of your skin. I admit to having made a few racist comments over the years but can anyone put their hand on their heart and say they haven't made similar comments? A few throwaway remarks, usually spoken in the heat of the moment, doesn't make you extreme right wing or a racist. What does make me laugh though: if you're right wing you are not just right wing – you are far right or extreme right. But if you are left wing you are only left wing, not extreme left or hard left. Funny that.

If I had to describe my politics I would say that I am a Loyalist. Loyal to the United Kingdom of Great Britain and Northern Ireland and to Her Majesty the Queen, who, to me, is the very best of British. I am also a proud Englishman and every time 23 April comes around, no matter where I am, I celebrate St George's Day. If I am at home I will normally have a drink with my old mate Dougie Trendle, aka Buster Bloodvessel from that great ska band Bad Manners. We have been pals for many years.

I am not into making a fuss about my birthday but St George's birthday is different. It is England's national day and for me it should be a public holiday. There can be no doubt that with the rise of English pride it is getting bigger and bigger so maybe one day we will get our holiday. It makes me sick when people go on about St Patrick's Day. It's the Plastic Paddies who give me the hump: just because they have taken their granny's auntie's dog for a walk they celebrate St Paddy's Day and not St George's Day. It should be the last thing anyone in England wants to celebrate. After all, they have been trying to blow us up for the last three hundred years!

There is nowhere that feels more British than Northern Ireland. I love going there on the twelfth of July for the anniversary of the Battle of the Boyne. It is blinding being with those good Loyalist people, many of whom I now class as friends. The whole thing is something special. I have been pulled by Special Branch a few times on my way over to Northern Ireland but I don't know if it is football-violence or paramilitary related. Either way it is a waste of their time because I ain't going there for either football or for paramilitary reasons.

My other great love is for Rangers; or the Blues Brothers as we call them. When I started following Chelsea I automatically affiliated to our bluenose pals in Glasgow. There are many of a Loyalist persuasion at Chelsea and we often go up there and they come down to Stamford Bridge. Due to Rangers going bust and being relegated to the third division, there are more and more of their lads coming down to watch Chelsea and over the years we have all become great friends.

One game we couldn't miss was Rangers–Aberdeen, at Ibrox, on 15 August 1986. Graeme Souness had been appointed as player-manager a few months before and this would be his first big game in that role. As Chelsea were playing Man United at Old Trafford the next day it meant we could kill two birds with one stone.

We left London in two minibuses on the Friday, just after the pubs closed, and drove all night. Our group included Chubby Chris and Darren Crewe. I remember walking into the District Bar on Paisley Road West at nine in the morning and ordering a pint. I just couldn't believe that Scotland's licensing laws allowed pubs to open at that time in the morning but I wasn't complaining. Thanks to our Loyalist leanings the Rangers supporters treated us really well. It was a home from home. I had a skinful and before I left the pub I was given a ticket by one of the Rangers boys.

Just going to watch the game was never going to be enough. Aberdeen had one of the best mobs in Britain and had a bitter rivalry with Rangers, matching the hatred between the two Old Firm clubs. We did our best to get into the away end but with our dress sense and accents we stood out like Jimmy Savile in a playground. The police were onto us in an instant and they weren't taking any prisoners.

This Jock Old Bill walked right up to me and stuck his ugly mug in my face.

'Dinnae bring your football violence here, you fucking English cunts. Keep it down the road.'

Charming. And if that wasn't enough he gave me a whack with his truncheon.

After the game, which Rangers won 2–0 – Souness scored too, even better – the drinking went on and on. Eventually, we ended up in an Orange lodge. I was no stranger to the lodge but for the other Chelsea lads it was an eye-opener, especially at the end of the night when everyone stood up for 'God Save the Queen'. That was the icing on the cake.

In the morning we went for breakfast, which in Scotland consists of those funny square sausages they eat up there, stuffed into bread rolls. With our hangovers in retreat we jumped into the minibus, which stank of sweat, fags and booze. It was time for Old Trafford.

When we got to the stadium there were lots of likely lads on the streets, from both sides. Now drunk again after a marathon session on the way down from Scotland our bus was very loud and we were all itching to have a go at United. It wasn't easy to get at them and the Manchester police were, as usual, being truncheon happy with anyone they suspected of being in a mob. We did manage to attack the Red Army outside Lou Macari's fish-and-chip shop but it was more of a scuffle than a battle and that was about all the action we saw that day.

What made the trip worthwhile was that we managed to beat Man U by a goal to nil. It was a major achievement for us because although we are rivals now we weren't then due to the huge gulf in class between the two sides.

Going back to Rangers, to me they are like the Loyalists in Northern Ireland: the best of British. Even the non-Scottish players who have played for them seem to get caught up in the Ibrox atmosphere. I will never forget Paul Gascoigne pretending to play the flute at Parkhead during an Old Firm match on 2 January 1998. Gazza had been named on the bench and was warming up when he got the treatment from Celtic fans: they pelted him with Mars bars and called him 'a fat Orange bastard'. So he gave them a few lines of 'The Sash' with that kid-on flute. Anything to do with the Orange

Walk is guarantee to infuriate the Soap Dodgers and coming from Gazza, a man they hated, made it even worse.

I loved his little celebration of Orangeism and I loved the way it annoyed the green-and-white brigade, who are so easy to wind up at the best of times. As someone once said, Celtic fans will go anywhere to be offended. There was also, as you might expect, a media outcry about what Paul did, which led to him getting fined £20,000 by Rangers and, more seriously, to death threats.

I have a tattoo on my thigh of Gazza playing the flute. As soon as I saw him doing it I had to get it done. It was my way of paying tribute to a man who is a real hero of mine. In 1990, to me, he was the best player in the world, a man with fantastic ability who almost took England into the World Cup final. I am gutted about his drink problems and desperate for him to pull through. Stay strong, Gazza.

Of course, I couldn't miss Rangers playing in the 2003 UEFA Cup final in Manchester. I went up there on my own but got together with my Stockport County pals, most of whom are good Loyalists. I also met Matthew Osbury and Andy Jane from Oxford, Shannon from Bristol City and John and Davie Duke from Edinburgh.

I went to savour the atmosphere, along with the estimated two hundred thousand other Rangers fans. If something went off fair enough, but that wasn't my main objective. I just wanted to celebrate Rangers and Loyalism and to watch the game on a big screen.

I was on a football ban at the time, and, although I had managed to get my hands on a ticket, according to the law I shouldn't have been allowed inside the stadium. Did I go to the match? What do you think? As for the trouble during the game – in Piccadilly, in the city centre – luckily for me I wasn't involved. I was probably somewhere else at the time!

* * *

It is not just in Northern Ireland that I have defended the cause of Loyalism. There is a big demo every year in London, organised by Troops Out, to commemorate the anniversary of Bloody Sunday. In 1972 the Parachute Regiment – heroes all – shot dead thirteen Catholics in Londonderry after coming under fire from IRA snipers. The Republicans see it as their annual opportunity to wallow in misery and promote their terrorist agenda.

MY LOVE FOR THE GERS

I have been on several counter-demos but the one that sticks in my mind took place in the late 1990s. There were many Chelsea there: PJ, Darren Crewe, Scottish Dave, Ian Holloway and Warren Glass and we were ably supported by others of a Loyalist persuasion. One thing, of course, united us, our hatred of the IRA and Republicanism. I would say there were about a hundred and twenty of us, but we were outnumbered by the thousands on the other side and that did not include those in their flute bands.

Of course it wasn't just Irish Republicans who were on the march. There were the usual left-wing scum as well; some from the Communist Party and suchlike along with a variety of unwashed, tree-hugging types from Save the Whale- and Save the Snail-type groups. We managed to ambush them outside the South African embassy, stopping them in their tracks. We hit a good few of them with bottles and other missiles. There was real hostility in the air, with the Fenians well up for a ruck, although most of the ones throwing the punches seemed to be from the far-left factions. My party piece was holding up the Irish tricolour and trying to set fire to the rag, an act that enraged the Republicans.

The main problem that day was that we had an informer in our ranks, who everyone now knows was Darren Wells. He has been interviewed on television about it and also gave an interview to the *Sunday Mirror* about his role. I wondered why the Old Bill were onto us so quickly, taking photos and names and addresses. Later I found out: they had been tipped off by someone who, to me, is one of the sneakiest, lowlife cunts I ever had the misfortune to know. Apart from anything else he put the kybosh on a good scrap, which is unforgiveable.

To be fair, although I never think of the tramp, people will never accept him because he is what he is and that's an informer. There's an old saying where I come from: every bit of grass gets cut.

No surrender.

24

It Was a Long Walk for Celtic

The air was rank with the smell of sectarian bile. This was different to any other game we were likely to be involved in. Tottenham, Man United, West Ham, we fucking hate the lot of them, but this was of a different order of magnitude. Why? Because thousands of IRA-supporting, terrorist-loving scum were in town.

That's right. We were playing Celtic at the Bridge.

I hate everything Celtic stand for, I hate their colours and I hate their former manager, Neil Lennon. Most of all I hate the murderers and gangsters of the Provisional IRA, people so callous that they planted bombs at war memorials when a service was taking place. They must have known that the likely outcome was the death of innocent women and children, but they didn't give a fuck.

I have never understood why fans of a British football team choose to fly the flag of Eire, a foreign country. When Celtic are playing all you see in the stadium is the Irish tricolour. I don't expect them to fly the Union Jack but there is never even a Scottish Saltire. Then there are the chants like, 'I, I, R, A, Irish Republican Army' and 'Ooh ah, Up the Ra'. If you're really unlucky they will give you the full songbook as well, from the Eire national anthem, 'A Soldier's Song', to the IRA hymn, 'The Boys of the Old Brigade'. When Celtic are playing away from home, the Fenian hordes swan around Scotland, taking over towns, intimidating the locals, causing mayhem. They get away with murder up there. Maybe they thought they could come down to London and rub our noses in it. No chance.

Chelsea won the Premier League title in season 2005/06, and Celtic, I hate to say it, won the Scottish equivalent, edging out my other team, Rangers. So some smart cunt thought it would be a good idea for the

English champions to take on the Scottish champions in a match to decide the unofficial British champions. The game was scheduled for 9 August 2006, with an evening kickoff.

I have never seen anything like it. Everyone wanted to get Celtic, not just Headhunters. We even had lads from other English mobs phoning us, every one of them desperate to take on the Paddies. As usual I was on a football ban but that wasn't going to keep me away. I got to the area around Stamford Bridge around two in the afternoon, where I ran into loads of Chelsea faces, including top boys like Hickey, Martin King and Kenny Goodwin. The early rumour was that Celtic had a big mob with them and that they were drinking in the Euston area.

As the excitement mounted, I bumped into the son of Brian Mason, who is a good pal of mine. Brian had just bought a pub called the White Hart (as it was then called) diagonally across from Fulham Broadway tube station, which is itself close to Stamford Bridge. Brian's son invited me in for a drink but the pub was empty. To help Brian out I say to his son, 'I can get this place mobbed out for you.' He was very grateful and promised to look after me. At any other time I would have rounded up our lads and pointed them towards the White Hart, earning myself a free drink or two in the process. But I was so focused on Celtic that I told him, 'To be honest I don't want a drink.'

Just at that moment, my phone went. 'Where are you?' one of our boys asked. It turned out there were a load of Fenians in Brogan's, which is just across from Fulham Broadway station. We were already in the White Hart when the Chelsea Youth ran into Brogan's, pulled out a Union Jack with 'Chelsea' on it and tore down their Irish tricolour.

There wasn't a word said. But what the Youth did raised the tension another notch, if that was possible. By this time we were lying in wait. There would be no backing down now, Old Bill or no Old Bill. Celtic would get what was coming to them, on behalf of every decent mob in Britain. We didn't have long to wait because from the depths of Fulham Broadway underground we could hear the unmistakeable strains of Irish Republican songs being belted out.

'Ooh ah, up the RAH,' was the cry.

It was the worst mistake they ever made.

We steamed across the road and smashed them to pieces.

Meanwhile Celtic were quickly ushered into Brogan's for their own safety by the police. Eventually, with the game about to kick off, they came out, escorted by a huge number of Old Bill. It wouldn't have mattered if the SAS had been guarding them; the result would have been the same. We pelted them with volleys of bricks, bottles and cans. And when we got through the ranks of Old Bill we steamed into the cunts, dishing out some heavy punishment. It was so bad that it took Celtic three-quarters of an hour to complete a walk that normally takes about three minutes.

It was the same after the game: bottles, bricks and charges. We were at it till midnight, ambushing them here, there and everywhere, with the cops unable to stop us. It brought back great memories. It was the Eighties all over again and I have never seen anything like it either before or since.

In the days after the game I put up a special section on my website. I wanted to thank the many people, from all over Britain – including a good number of the Blues Brothers from Rangers – who had turned out to attack Celtic. I also made what I think was a good point: when Celtic had been playing Fulham they brought more than ten thousand with them. For us, it was three thousand. Maybe that extra mile from Fulham made it too far to travel!

In my honest opinion that night was miles in front of the Cardiff game. Sporadic violence at its best. We took them and the Old Bill by surprise. I don't think they'll be in a hurry to play that fixture again.

25

Other Firms

Every club in England has a firm (the small clubs are probably the most active these days) and I could probably talk about all ninety-two of them. These, however, are my particular favourites.

Tottenham

I hate them with a passion, the team, the supporters, the area, the stadium, the lack of a Tube station. I might be contradicting myself, but that doesn't mean I don't have some good pals who are Spurs fans. In fact I have friends at most clubs, despite the fact that Chelsea is one of those clubs that everyone hates. One of Tottenham's main faces is Rob Campbell, who, despite his dodgy Scottish surname, is a good mate of mine.

To be fair we have had some really good battles with them over the years. Their hatred for us, and ours for them, will never end. If you are caught up in the scene no other team will compare to the hatred we feel for each other. Their firm detest us with a passion. To me, that says we are doing something right, whether it's on or off the field.

One thing that annoys me about them is that they never admit getting done. I know I go on about the Battle of Parsons Green, when we done them, but this is my book and I am telling the truth. They have always been the same and I don't understand why.

I don't mind admitting I was there at the Ifield tavern when they came round and smashed the place to smithereens. Sometimes, whether you like it or not, you have to give credit where it's due. It's part of being a grown-up mob.

Arsenal

A lot of Chelsea lads dislike Arsenal, but I have some good pals there. I am not saying I want them to win but I haven't got that same hatred for them, the way I have for Spurs or Celtic. They have never really been mentioned and I wouldn't say they have the best mob in the world. But if you come across them they will have a row. They are not there just for show.

West Ham

There will always be rivalry between us and the Marshmen, as we call them. Every time you talk to a West Ham fan they are all related to the Krays and have taken Ronnie and Reggie's auntie's dog for a walk. No wonder the Krays got so many Christmas cards in Broadmoor; half the East End were their cousins or uncles. Fuck me.

But I have to be fair. Until Hickey came along and took us by the scruff of the neck, the ICF were the most organised firm in the country bar none, and they deserve respect for that. With their calling cards and battle plans they took hooliganism to a new level, although in later years I think we caught them up and then surpassed them. They are a bit like us and the Yids: there is no middle ground and if you don't support them you will hate them.

Like Tottenham they also don't like to admit when they are run. When I became good pals with Cass Pennant and Carlton Leach, I got to know about the times they were turned over.

Talking about Carlton, I now do shows with him. He has become a very close friend. There is mutual respect there and we really enjoy each other's company. We have had some great times together, and, whether people like it or not, that's a fact. He has also written a book and the film *Rise of the Footsoldier* is based on his life. Carlton is a lucky man. The night his pal Tony Tucker got shot dead – in the so-called 'Range Rover killings' – he didn't call on Carlton or he would also have taken a bullet.

I have also done gigs with Cass. I believe some people are a little bit jealous of the way he has turned his life around and is now doing well. It's funny the way it has turned out, me working with Carlton and Cass. At one time we would have been at each other's throats, but now we are mates.

I still hope West Ham go down though.

Millwall

Their rendition of the line, 'No one likes us, we don't care,' is the best I have ever heard. It is sung with such venom, hatred and raw passion. And they are fucking right because no one does like them (although once again I have to admit to having a few pals down that way). We have had some great rows with them over the years; they got some good results against us, but we also got some good ones against them.

I remember 1995 in the FA Cup. It was a Saturday game and we met in the Hercules pub, Lambeth North. It was early, opening time. Millwall were in the Gregorian, Jamaica Road, one of their pubs. By their own admission, they didn't have the numbers they were expecting but we knew that the mob they had in there was tooled up and up for it. We wanted to get off at Borough tube station and walk down to the Greg but the Old Bill spoiled our dream. They rounded us up and put us back on the train, which took us straight to the Den.

When we arrived there were a few skirmishes with Millwall and after the game there were a few more. Not great news for the Old Bill but there was a replay at Stamford Bridge. On the night we were full of anticipation and there were constant fights in and around the ground. To be fair Millwall's mob were better at our place than they were at their own.

I can just imagine the Old Bill with their heads in their fucking hands when Chelsea and Millwall are drawn together in a cup competition. Despair doesn't even come close.

Chelsea versus Millwall. The fixture says it all.

Sheffield United

I got bottled in a pub called Berlins in Sheffield and had to go to hospital to get stitches. It was 7 May 1994, the last game of the season, and we won 3–2, sending them down. It all kicked off in Berlins a few hours after the game, with one of our boys, Flynny (a well-known Sheffield Wednesday fan who used to come to Chelsea in the early days) even getting bitten outside the boozer by a dog.

Their firm has always been top class and we have had many offs with them. The fight in Berlins was payback for a battle in Camden Town when we absolutely slaughtered them. I have got to know many of their boys, in particular Steve Cowens, who wrote the book *Blades Business Crew: the Inside Story of a Football Hooligan Gang*, which of course is the story of their mob. They are all good lads who go abroad a lot with England. Steve even arranged for me to do a show up there and there must have been two hundred of their boys there on the night. I was treated with the utmost respect and for that I take my hat off to them. Let's face it, that sort of fraternisation with the enemy would never have happened a few years ago.

Notts Forest

They have always had a good mob and they also travel regularly with England. Although they are not so well known for going to away games in domestic football, we have had many a tussle with the Forest Executive Crew, as they are known, although with no disrespect there is not the same level of hatred for them that we have for some of the bigger clubs. Gary 'Boatsy' Clarke (who wrote their book) is the top boy in the Nottingham neck of the woods and he has been a friend for many years.

In 1985, at Earl's Court, we had a proper toe-to-toe with Forest. To be fair they did quite well but we were too strong for them. All the same, we respected them for turning up and having a go.

Middlesbrough

Quite simply, they are the best Northern mob I have ever seen. There have been so many turnouts with them: at the 1988 playoffs, home and away; at the Full Members Cup final; in the Three Kings pub in North End Road in the 1997 FA Cup (when Di Matteo scored); at Kingsbury on the platform. Game mob.

Leeds

Leeds has a good Loyalist following and they are also very proud of their area, so fair play to them for that. They are also no shrinking violets and there have been some memorable clashes with us. One of the best was on 15 May 2004, our last home game of the season, which we won 1–0. Leeds were in the White Horse at Parsons Green with a huge mob but they were hemmed in by Old Bill. I thought it was going to be a non-event but eventually they gave the cops the slip and there was an outstanding off.

I also recall going to Leeds on Hickey's coach in the 1980s. We got off at Pudsey, three coach loads of us, six miles from the city centre. We then marched into Leeds, not having a fucking clue where they were or how many. When we got there we confronted them and had a right battle.

Those were the days though: no mobile phones, no internet; no keyboard warriors. We also had a very good day – we beat them 5–0 I think – when they came to us and smashed our scoreboard to bits.

Birmingham City

My pal Paul Tait used to play for them. Paul got an amazing amount of publicity when he scored a golden goal (was it the first ever golden goal?) in the 1995 Auto Windscreens Shield final. It wasn't so much the goal but the fact that he pulled up his strip and revealed a T-shirt underneath that read 'Shit on the Villa'.

I thought you might enjoy that little story but now it's time for more violence. The Birmingham mob, the Zulu Warriors, have always been able to pull good numbers and have it. They are good on their day. Their top boys – Barrington, Brains and Spencer McCracken – are as good as anyone in the country, and yes, you've guessed it, they are also good pals of mine! That doesn't mean we haven't clashed. I remember a good go in the Bull Ring in Birmingham city centre, and also walking to their ground and them coming out of the side streets in the pitch dark and bricking us.

They would never pass up the chance of a row, even when they weren't playing. In the late 1980s, we met Manchester United at Villa Park in a cup semi-final but ended up fighting the Zulus. There was also trouble in the Elusive Camel in Pimlico: Tony Covelle sent Perky into the pub to spy on them because of his so-called Brummie accent. I couldn't help laughing. 'He's from Skegness you cunt. Not Birmingham,' I told him.

Wolves

As I said earlier I got done there as a young kid, an event that made me a Headhunter for life after the way our boys went looking for the cunts who did it. Despite what happened I have grown to respect the Wolves mob, simply because they have always pulled good numbers. I have also become very friendly with a lot of them – the likes of Nick Guy, Mini, Abbos, Gilly, Spats and Lawly.

My good pals, Matthew Lemm and Dean Greatrex, put on a show for me up there. Danny Dyer was my guest and ninety of the Wolves mob turned up, along with another two hundred and fifty punters. A great turnout. 'Fuck me,' I said to them. 'Do you think you are playing Birmingham today?'

Bristol City

You are always guaranteed a row in the well-known area of St Paul's if that's what you are looking for and of course we always were. Chelsea have had some good battles there over the years.

Burnley

A proper Northern town that has some diehard and game lads, many of whom I have met through England. We had them in a pre-season game, round about the time of the Mosside riots in 1981. Take it from me you have never seen so many Old Bill at Euston at eight o'clock in the morning. That speaks volumes about Burnley's reputation and capability.

Stoke

They are one of the only mobs who have tried to take liberties at Stamford Bridge. A few years ago a minibus load of them took us on at the Elm pub down the North End Road. They came unstuck but you have to give credit where credit is due because they are one of the few firms who are always up for it.

Man United

They are disliked everywhere they go. You have to admit that is because they have been a great football team that has won a lot of trophies. When you win people are bound to be jealous and, quite naturally, they will hate you for being so successful.

No doubt due to the size of their fanbase, mob wise they have always travelled well and we have had some good battles with them in London, for example at the Lion and Lamb pub at Euston. I was also very impressed by the sheer size of a mob they had this day on North End Road.

Their decision to dress all in black for a game against an Italian team – if memory serves – was a good one. From that day on the name 'Men in Black' was their copyright. I just thought these cunts look so stylish representing England.

Man City

At one Friday night televised game against City we ran fucking riot in Manchester. There were thousands of Chelsea there and City have admitted we took liberties that night. The Full Members Cup final at Wembley in 1986 was another great battle; at every corner you turned it was going off, not to mention the battles in the car parks, on Wembley Way and inside the stadium itself. In the early 2000s we met them in an end-of-season relegation decider at Stamford Bridge and the fighting spilled onto the pitch.

I respect City as a mob and also because they follow England well. I know Trav, Macca and Sykesy through England and we have been friends for a long time.

I could go on and on about teams that deserve respect, including mobs from smaller clubs, the likes of Lincoln for example. They can be just as dedicated as the lads from big clubs.

26

Lansdowne Road and the National Anthem

The Republic of Ireland, in Dublin, at Lansdowne Road, where the British national anthem had never been played, where anti-English feeling still runs as high as it does anywhere in the world. That was one match no true England fan was ever going to miss. And I am a true England fan. The papers had been hyping it up for weeks. They could smell trouble and we weren't about to disappoint them.

The press was right. Given the circumstances across the water, it was almost inevitable there would be trouble. It was February 1995 and the political situation in Ulster was still very tense. There was a strong feeling in Northern Ireland that John Major, the then prime minister, was selling the Protestant people of Ulster down the river with his so-called peace process. On the back of the peace talks the IRA had declared a ceasefire, in August 1994, just a few months before the game, but none of us believed a word of it. (We were right not to believe it because just a few months later, in August 1995, Sinn Fein leader Gerry Adams said to a mass rally in Belfast that the Provos 'haven't gone away, you know'.) The men in balaclavas were still a threat and if they didn't get their way they would quickly take up arms again. If we didn't achieve anything else we could at least put on a show of support for our Loyalist friends.

I was a Category C football hooligan and would be hounded by journalists and police from both sides of the Irish Sea. They were sure to be watching Heathrow closely so I decided to go from Stansted. The Stansted ploy didn't work because as soon as I got to check-in I was being followed by reporters and photographers. This was going to be even more high-profile than I thought.

When I got to Dublin I met quite a few Chelsea, including Andy Garner and Disco, both from Stockport/Chelsea, and a lot of lads from other clubs, among them Maggie, Swiggy and Andy Turner from Stockport County and Trav from Man City. In the aftermath of the game I read that the England fans in Dublin were more 'hardcore' than usual and that is spot on. We were also more Loyalist and anti-IRA than usual.

After a quick drink my main priority was to get a ticket for the game. I also wanted to get into the ground early so that I didn't miss the British national anthem being played: I was going to sing it with pride, as I always did. When I got onto O'Connell Street I realised that getting into the game might not be that easy. There were hundreds of England who had travelled without tickets and like me they were on the hunt for one.

We were all heading to catch the train to Lansdowne Road and as we walked we were belting out the national anthem as well as 'No Surrender to the IRA', neither of which, I assure you, made us very popular on the streets of Dublin. We got to the station but for some reason found ourselves on the wrong platform. No problem: we walked across the tracks, much to the disgust of the Dubliners who were coming home from work. We didn't win any popularity contests on the train going out to Lansdowne Road either. It was a busy commuter service and by the time we got on board it was so packed that we were sweating like Harold Shipman in the dock.

Those commuters got the shock of their lives. Hundreds of smartly dressed thugs, stinking of drink, singing and chanting. We serenaded them with 'Fuck the Pope and the IRA', and when we got off at the stadium we launched into the national anthem. No one came near us, not even the Gardai, who stared at us in amazement. I don't think they had ever come across anything quite like it.

There was an hour to go before kickoff but, much to our disappointment, there was no one to have it with. So I decided to put all my efforts into getting a ticket. Some of my mates had one and they went into the stadium, but there were hundreds of us who didn't and we were struggling to find touts. As we were hell bent on getting in we came up with a plan. 'We ain't come this far for nothing. We'll just have to jump the turnstile. Whoever makes it makes it,' I said.

England fans were by now streaming through the waist-high turnstiles. We joined in. Some jumped over the turnstiles, some went in by sticking like glue to the bloke in front; others passed their ticket back. I managed to get in but there were stewards on the other side and they were searching everyone. One of the hi-viz brigade made himself busy as I was passing and he shouted to the Gardai Old Bill that I didn't have a ticket.

The cops grabbed a hold of me and marched me out of the stadium. I knew that the next stop was the back of a police van. Luckily for me the concourse outside was now full of England lads, some of the gamest and most aggressive around, many of whom I knew. Seeing me being led away they did not hesitate. They steamed into the Gardai, which allowed me to melt away into the crowds.

I was still determined to get inside, and, eventually, I found a tout. He sold me a ticket for the Ireland end behind the goals and although I was over the moon when I passed through the turnstile I realised there was still a problem: I would have to spend the whole ninety minutes surrounded by the Tea Caddies. That was never going to happen so I wriggled my way down to the front of the terracing, as close as possible to the England section, which was now to my left. I would wait for the right moment and then make my move.

The next thing was that the British national anthem starts up. Quite naturally, the England fans sing it loudly and with pride while the rest of the ground try to drown it out with boos and whistles. This one Paddy near to me was really cunting us off.

'You dirty pin-pulling cunt,' I growled.

In a single manoeuvre I punched him in the face and jumped over the perimeter wall at the side of the pitch. He tried to hit me back and other Irish started to abuse me but by this time I was walking away from them and towards the England section. A steward approached me and I said, 'Listen mate. I'm English. I'm in the wrong end.' He didn't question how I had got there; he just escorted me into our part of the ground.

So far, so good.

There had been a few skirmishes when the national anthems were played but nothing to write home about. That all changed when Ireland scored about twenty minutes into the game. I was in the lower tier, where we were next to Irish fans and as soon as the goal went in the Tea Caddies in another part of the stadium started with 'Ooh ah, up the RAH'. That was it, the proverbial red rag to a bull. We steamed into the fuckers.

At the same time the top tier of the stand, which was all England, started to rip up seats and throw them at the Irish, along with a hail of coins, bottles and cans. Their aim wasn't too good because some of the missiles hit us. The press – who we also attacked – had a field day, claiming that it was the upper tier who were the instigators but that was wrong: it was the lads down below who kicked it off. I bet you can't believe the media got it wrong!

The Gardai joined in, attacking us but not their fellow countrymen. Within a short space of time the fighting spilled onto the pitch, forcing the Dutch referee to take the teams off the pitch. The game was then abandoned, which to me was ludicrous because to be quite honest I have seen much, much worse at football.

The next day the media, the authorities and the politicians – the usual suspects – proclaimed themselves outraged at what had happened, making a mountain out of a fucking molehill. *The Times*, the newspaper of the establishment, got on its high horse: 'English football was plunged into its worst crisis since the Heysel disaster ten years ago when thirty-nine Italian fans died during the European Cup final between Liverpool and Juventus.'

What a load of bollocks. Let's look at the casualty list from Lansdowne Road: twenty people, including stewards and police, were injured, with one of them getting his skull broken; one Irish fan, in his sixties, died of a heart attack as the ground was being evacuated but that was due to natural causes and had nothing to do with the fighting; a few seats got ripped up. How does that compare to thirty-nine dying at Heysel? It doesn't.

It didn't stop the hysteria, with some papers even suggesting that the 1996 European Championships might be taken away from England. The politicians weighed in with their tuppence worth, with John Major calling the England fans 'a disgrace and an embarrassment'. The blame game then got into full swing with the English police claiming that they had told the Irish Old Bill about the likelihood of trouble by organised groups – including the National Front and Combat 18 – in the run-up to the match. The Gardai denied it and pointed out that they had six hundred cops on duty on the night, many of them in full riot gear.

As I said I have seen much worse at football but the fact it was such a high-profile game in the middle of important political negotiations meant that what happened was always going to be exaggerated. But, that said, it was an away win because we gave the Irish a beating and wrecked large parts of their ground.

The next day I flew home with about three hundred other England. When I got to Stansted there were three official-looking cunts on duty. One had a question for me.

'Where have you just come from?'

'As the plane has just landed from Dublin, I would imagine Dublin. Wouldn't you?'

'What did you go to Dublin for?'

'For pleasure.'

'Did you go to the football?'

'If that comes under pleasure, then yes.'

'What is your club team?'

'I don't follow a club.'

One of the three walked away and a couple of minutes later came back. He wrote something on a piece of paper and put it face down. They then told me they were football-intelligence officers and had reason to believe I was involved in trouble in the England section at Lansdowne Road, which was what the media had focused on. Then one of them went on with the interrogation.

'Can I search you?'

'Yes.'

'Have you got anything on you shouldn't have?'

'Yes, you.'

As he takes my coat off he notices that I have massive Chelsea tattoos.

'I thought you didn't support a club,' he said.

'I can't believe someone put them on me.'

The copper who had come back with the piece of paper then turned it over. It read: 'Jason Marriner, Chelsea. Known Headhunter. Category C.'

The implication was that I had instigated a lot of the trouble. That was obvious. Of the three hundred faces on that plane only one other person got interrogated. Obviously, they didn't like the look of me and were trying to pin the whole fucking thing on me. In these situations it is important to keep your wits about you and not to panic. Then it came to me, divine inspiration if you like.

'Could you repeat where the trouble was and where you thought I was?' I asked in my most helpful and constructive tone.

They said they didn't have to tell me exactly where I was but it was in the England section.

It was time for me to play the winning hand.

'I think you will find you've got the wrong man.'

I pulled out my ticket. It was, of course, for the Ireland end.

'How could I have been in two places at once? That is impossible.'

Their facial expressions said it all. They were fucking gutted.

I walked through customs and went home.

Two-nil to England in my book. And this is my book, so two-nil it is.

27

Paying the Price

I got nicked for Cardiff months after the game, when they had gone through loads of footage from CCTV. No charges were laid and I was bailed pending further enquiries. It was then a question of waiting for them to come through your door one day at fuck-off o'clock in the morning. Sure enough, months later, they came to arrest me at half-six one morning, complete with television crew. But it was the wrong house because by that time I had moved. They did the same thing with Andy Frain and would eventually widen the net to arrest a total of ninety-six people.

Given that they missed me the first time they decided to send an email via my website with words to the effect of 'hand yourself in or we're coming through your door'. I suppose, apart from anything else, it's cheaper and less time consuming. As I knew they had already been to my old gaff I phoned my solicitor, who got in touch with the Old Bill. I met him at the police station and after briefing him on a few things we went inside. They showed me DVDs and asked all the questions you might expect but I kept schtum. I never even gave them a 'no comment' because I have the right to remain silent and so I always remain silent, as I have said before.

I was released on police bail and told to come back this day when I would be informed if I was going to be charged. I thought: '*If I was going to be charged.*' That was a joke. It was always going to happen and, of course, it did. My next stop was West London magistrates' court in Hammersmith, as it would be for a lot more Chelsea.

It was a really hot day for the court case. I turned up, along with fifty-three of our lads. As I walked in one of my mates seemed rather surprised.

'Aren't you due in court today, Jase?'

I looked at him. 'I am in court. What are you talking about?'

He was amazed. 'You can't go into court looking like that.'

I was wearing a T-shirt, shorts and flip-flops while he had his smartest suit on. My reason for dressing like that was because it was hot and, let's face it, I was the one who would get put away not the suit. I also pointed out to my mate this was by way of a preliminary hearing.

'We're in magistrates' court. One's a dentist, one's a chiropodist. The other owns a sweet shop. This is going to drag on for ages. I wouldn't worry about it.'

I was on my phone in front of the court, taking a call from a mate. 'Rosie Cheeks', the football-intelligence spotter at Chelsea, walked past.

'All right, Jase?' he said.

I asked my pal to hold on for a minute.

'Fucking all right Jase? My mates call me Jase. You are the cunt behind all of this. You spotters are all two-faced.'

I was going to end up in the warehouse because of him and he wants to know if I am all right. Fuck me!

Nothing happened on the day, apart from us being told that we would be sent to the Crown Court for trial at a later date. You can plead guilty or not guilty but there is also the possibility of entering a response of no-indication, which I did. Not many people are aware of it but it lets you sit on the fence for a while by not letting the prosecution know which way you are going. But in the end I was always likely to go for not guilty, a decision that I put a great deal of thought into and one that was guided by my experience of the criminal-justice system.

The judge in the Crown Court, the Honourable Edmonds, was presiding over everything to do with the case, for both Chelsea and Cardiff. He had given us sentencing guidelines: for a guilty plea I would get a minimum of two years four months, while the maximum possible was five years. If I opted for not guilty I would be looking at, say, three years. It was a gamble but in my head I thought I would get two years if found guilty, even though Judge Edmonds had decreed a minimum of two years four months. But I knew they didn't always go with the guidelines and what I had done didn't warrant a day let alone a two-stretch. Anyway, I might be able to appeal a longer sentence on the grounds that it was out of proportion to the seriousness of my offence.

The other factor was the 'West Ham Rolex' and how it played into sentencing decisions. With a two-year term I would be out with a tag after ten months while for three years it would be fifteen months inside and then out with the tag. So I calculated that I was gambling with five months of my life and that a not-guilty plea was worth the risk.

There were so many defendants that the whole process had to split into groups of five or six, which meant there would be twelve trials for Chelsea alone. With my status as a Category C hooligan, my previous and my alleged prominence on the day in question I am number one on the indictment in the first trial. Alongside me in the dock were Muggsy, Carl from Rugby, Vodka John, John Devitt and Mickey Garrity. I don't think they were best pleased at being on trial with me: with the amount of form I've got they were obviously afraid of being tarred with the same brush. To be honest I don't blame them – I wouldn't want to be on trial with me either, simply because of my form.

The trial opens with the prosecution making a statement about me being infamous and that the jury must not look me up on the internet. Fuck me, I thought, what a load of bollocks: as soon as they get home they will be straight onto the computer, typing 'Jason Marriner, Chelsea' into Google. And even if they don't, the fact that I have been labelled 'notorious' by the prosecution is hardly going to help me get a fair trial.

When I got into the witness box a few days later, the old chocolate fudge weighed in, firmly instructing the jury that on no account should anyone look me up. As usual I couldn't contain myself: 'Well, if you've turned and told them not to look on the internet your honour then of course they won't,' I told him in my best piss-taking tone. Then, with a smile, I added: 'I think it's a little too late your honour. I think they would have done it days ago.'

In the period between the start of the trial and me going into the dock I did a little plan of the judge and jurors. The judge I put down as a silent assassin and then I challenged the rest of the lads to pick out the person they thought would be elected head juror – for £5 a head. Well I had to do something to ward off the boredom. Another ploy to liven things up was singing to the Old Bill when I was being taken in and out of the dock. 'Please release me, let me go,' I sang, or 'Don't leave me this way.' Well, you've got to have a bit of a laugh, haven't you?

When the trial opened they showed a DVD of the fight with Cardiff and I will never forget the expression on the face of the female juror at the end of the front row. Her mouth was wide open. She was disgusted.

I nudged Muggsy. 'There's one guilty already in the first ten minutes.'

Under cross examination the prosecuting barrister puts it to me that I am 'famous', or as he would probably prefer it, 'infamous'.

'They are your words sir. I don't believe I am either.'

Having started on the famous/infamous tack he wasn't about to let it go.

'You have written a book, been in a film, you've got a DVD out, you've been in documentaries.'

Then he turned to the jury.

'I am sure the jury would agree with me you are one of the two.'

With that attempt at persuasion, he faced me again.

'On the morning of the Cardiff game you were selling DVDs and books down the Fulham Road.'

'Well that don't make me famous or infamous. If you sign my book that doesn't make you famous,' I retorted.

For a moment, I wasn't sure what the fuck he was getting at with all the questions about me being famous. Then it dawned on me. He was arguing that anyone with my profile would stick out like a sore thumb and so it would be unlikely that witnesses would mistake me for someone else. I told him that as I hadn't done anything wrong I couldn't see what the problem was.

We moved onto a viewing of the DVD made by the Old Bill. He showed me before the game and then after it. I had changed my hat and coat to avoid being recognised, he said. I told him it was nothing to do with that: it was cold and the weather kept changing, I pointed out.

The next clip was of me at the front of our firm. I batted that one away as well.

'So what. Someone has to be first and someone has to be last. It's like the queue in the fish-and-chip shop.'

'You always seem to be first,' he noted.

'Well I am always first in the fish-and-chip shop,' I said, as I patted my stomach.

He then accusing me of leading a mob down Holmesdale Road.

'No, the police pushed us down that road,' which of course was true.

He then shouted quite loudly, no doubt trying to convey his mock outrage to the jury.

'Are you blaming the police for what happened on this day?'

'Why are you shouting at me? I am only two yards away from you. I ain't in Bermondsey. That's exactly what I am saying. I *am* blaming the police.'

He looked astonished at this answer. He could not believe it.

'What do you mean? That's an outrageous accusation.'

So I told him exactly what I meant.

'A few weeks ago I watched Liverpool play Man U at Old Trafford and after the game I was listening to Jamie Redknapp and they kept 1,800 Scousers in for half an hour after the game. So I believe the Old Bill was either incompetent or was just out for a plain out-and-out stitch-up. Why would you let six thousand Cardiff supporters out at the same time as Chelsea?'

I believed what I was telling him and to this day I still do. Today the police let you get on with it, film you and then nick you. It wasn't a schoolboy error. It was what they wanted.

The cross-examination wasn't getting anywhere. I was blaming the police and I was also telling him I would like to know what I was doing in this courtroom, because I genuinely didn't know. To be honest, of course, if they had filmed me down the Fulham Road, where I smacked a Welsh geezer, they would have had me bang to rights.

He also said that I was a very confident person in the dock and asked if that was down to my after-dinner talks.

'No, I don't believe so. I am confident because I haven't done anything wrong. But you must come to one of my after-dinner talks because I am sure you would enjoy yourself.'

I think my inquisitor enjoyed our little sparring sessions. To me he had a real spring in his step as he strutted up and down the court. I thought he was trying to copy one of those lawyers you see in television dramas, so I said to him at one point: 'This is all very dramatic isn't it? I think you have watched too much television.' While later on I remarked, 'I think you're jealous of me because you're a failed actor. You would love to be in DVDs and documentaries.'

When all the evidence had been heard we then had to wait for the jury's verdict. It took them a day and a half to deliberate but there were six of us on trial, me for violent disorder and the other five on the lesser charge of affray. Finally, they filed back into their seats and we were asked to stand up. They find me guilty.

'Now there's a surprise,' I say, smiling broadly at the twelve people who have just convicted me. It was hardly a surprise. In my heart of hearts I always knew I was going to get a guilty verdict. As for the others, Muggsy gets a guilty, as do Micky Garrity and John Devitt. Both Carl from Rugby and Vodka John both get found not guilty and when this is announced I shout 'yes!' My outburst startled the jury, but I did it because it was us against the system. It was an away win.

At that point, the two not-guilty lads leave the dock and the Honourable Judge Edmonds says he wants background reports on Muggsy, Nicky and John but not on me. He then grants us bail for seven weeks, pending sentencing. I immediately realise that I have a one-way ticket to the warehouse so I call over my barrister and tell him I refuse bail. I wanted to get started right away, not to wait seven weeks. The quicker I am in the quicker I am out.

Muggsy looks at me and says, 'We are going to the pub.'

'I hope you have a stinking hangover in the morning,' I tell him and with that they leave the dock while I walk down to the cells before being whisked off to the Scrubs.

Of course the media had a field day. *The Sun*'s coverage was typical. Under a headline of 'The End of a Reign of Terror' it wrote that, 'For decades the mere mention of their name struck fear and terror into the hearts of football fans across the UK and Europe. They revelled in being the most notorious hooligans on the planet. They were the Chelsea Headhunters.'

They were right about one thing but wrong about another. Yes we were the most feared firm in football but, no, it was not an end to the reign of terror. I will come back to that later.

In the meantime, I was back in the old routine.

28

Nick the Penny Chew

I hadn't seen him for twelve years, not since I had last done a bit of bird. But I would have recognised that boat anywhere. Fuck me, if it wasn't Nick 'the Jew' Kutner. He was on the landing below, making a cuppa for the screws, as he had been the last time we were behind the door together.

I couldn't resist it. 'You still making tea for the kangas, Nick?'

He handed the tea to the screws and I went down from the 'threes' to the 'twos' to have a word.

'Not football violence again, Jase,' he said in that posh voice of his.

I fired back right away. 'I bet you're in here for fucking fraud again.'

'About time you gave that up,' he said.

'About time you give the fraud up. You're obviously no good at it.'

Just after I got to know Nick, and going on his surname, I asked him a question.

'Are you and your family Jewish?'

'Yes.'

I told him I had some sore memories of Auschwitz and that it deeply saddened me what happened to my granddad there.

'Why? What happened to him?' he asked.

As I walked away I told him: 'My granddad died there. I can't bring myself to talk about it at the moment.'

A couple of days had gone by when I said to him:

'I think we've got crossed wires about my granddad getting killed. It was his own fault.'

'Why?'

'He went to work pissed and fell out of the watchtower.'

Nick loved that one.

'You cunt,' he laughed.

I was on C wing, Wormwood Scrubs, which is mainly used for remand prisoners but has some convicted men on there too. The 'Penny Chew' had obviously got well in with the screws, as he always did, making sure he got the cushtiest number in the place. I wouldn't have made tea for the cunts, but that was his chosen job and he didn't care what people thought. His attitude was that none of the cons are his friends and he wanted to make his bird as easy as possible and get out at the earliest possible opportunity. I understood where he was coming from and making tea is an easy job. It is just that, on a point of principle, I wouldn't ever do that job, although there are some all right screws.

You could make a film out of Nick's life. To call him a colourful character would be the understatement of the century. Take his background. As the *Daily Telegraph* reported, 'Nicholas Kutner was raised in a world of privilege and given opportunities that most people could only dream of.' Growing up, he lived with his family in a mansion flat overlooking Regent's Park – a 'millionaire's row', as one paper described it – and was sent to an expensive private school. His mum and dad even mixed with royalty for fuck's sake.

His problem was always gambling and when the bug got hold of him he 'began his descent into a life of crime,' as the press would no doubt put it. Nick became a conman and stacked up a huge amount of convictions for fraud. Then in November 2013 he faced a charge that could have put him away for life: murder. You will remember the Carole Waugh case, the wealthy woman who worked as an escort because she was lonely. The prosecution alleged that Nick and his associate, Rakesh Bhayani, murdered her so that they could steal her money and spend it on gambling.

Bhayani was convicted of murder and although Nick got found not guilty on that charge he was done for perverting the course of justice and fraud. His sentence was longer than some people get for murder – thirteen years. He will need all his experience of the system to get through that one.

Back to the present.

Nick asked me if there was anything I needed or wanted. I told him I wanted a job ASAP to get me out of my cell. I knew he would have a cheeky word with the Kangas and also that they would see from my 'page 16' (a dossier on a prisoner with a profile of things like: what he is in for, who he associates with, whether he is a junkie) that I didn't use drugs. The screws like a quiet life and don't want to be running after you so if they can trust you to get on with it they are happy.

I had already got my cell and wing sorted to my satisfaction. Once again it was thanks to my knowledge of the system. During my time in the induction wing there was a black lad there called Manny, with whom I got on well. 'Do you think we could get banged up together?' he asked me. I knew the score. The screws, always trying to minimise potential problems, were keen to keep you happy and if that meant giving you a cell with one of your mates that was fine by them. What you had to do was speak up.

Manny and I queued up outside the office, where they tell you which cell you are going in. 'Can I bang up with him, guv?' I asked the screw behind the desk. So they let Manny and I share. I walk into the cell first and tell Manny he has to take the top bunk as I am scared of heights. I am of course taking the piss but the end result was that I got the bottom bunk. 'I got to have you as my pad-mate as someone's got to turn the telly over,' I tell him.

A few days later a screw came to my door and tells me I am moving to the 'twos' on the opposite side of C-wing. My new cell is next door to a pal of mine, Jeff Majors, which is quite handy because we would cook each other curries we made in our kettles and pass them out the window to each other. Manny however did not move with me so my new pad-mate is Wayne 'Robbo' Roberts.

A week later I get offered a voluntary cleaning job in the 'seg' (segregation wing), which is a good job, but one that I turn down because I want to go to the gym and workout when it is gym day. The problem is that the seg job clashes with gym days. I put Robbo's name forward for the job, which meant he would have to move to a new wing. But, at the end of the day, it's all about making your sentence as easy as possible and helping each other out.

Lackey, my mate, was number one on the hotplate, which is in the servery. He kept going to the kangas and telling them, 'We want Jason to work on the hotplate.' He knows I am a good laugh and that I get on well with the lads who work on the servery but I know from my previous sentence that the hotplate is more trouble than it's worth. You think Oliver Twist was always hungry and asking for more – try serving those one-eyed junkie cunts. Prisoners always want more: more chips, more potatoes, more of fucking everything. If you've got a mate on the server he will try and slip you something later but not in front of everyone.

Eventually, my number comes up and I get a job as a landing cleaner. By prison standards I am well pleased. The job is fairly cushty and not too stressful and I have the added bonus of having Manny back as my cell-mate, on the twos (and yes, he is still in the top bunk!).

I am chipping away nicely at my days, and I am also in a position to help the other Chelsea lads who by now are arriving. Some of them had no experience of doing time so I knew I needed to help them through the whole thing. When I am on my rounds I try to help. Craig McGuire, one of our Youth (I say Youth but at the time he was about 25), was in there. He's a good lad and took his sentence like a man. It was his first bit of bird so I tried to help him with a paper through his door, a little thing but actually a big help.

29

To Me, He Is 'The Mongrel'

Seven weeks after refusing bail, on 24 March 2011, I was taken from the Scrubs back to Crown Court for sentencing. While I am in the court cells downstairs my barrister comes down to see me with my solicitor's clerk. The clerk is there to take notes for my solicitor, who is in the courtroom. She gives me a head's up on what is going on above us.

'It is absolutely mobbed up there. You couldn't get another person in. I have to tell you this. *He's* there.'

'Who's there?'

I didn't have a clue who she was talking about.

'MacIntyre.'

I couldn't stop laughing

'What does that cunt want?'

I thought, 'Twelve years after the documentary and he is still trying to live off me'. To me, he is a dog: apart from anything else, what undercover journalist goes on *Come Dine with Me*?

My co-defendants are already in court waiting for me to come up the stairs and as I join them in the dock I shake everyone's hand. The solicitor's clerk had told me that MacIntyre had already been threatened inside and outside the building and for that reason had two burly cozzers by his side. I didn't give a fuck where he was or who he was with. I was about to give the man I think of as 'the Mongrel' a bit of stick.

As I walk round to take my seat I realise that the clerk hadn't been exaggerating. The place really is packed. With barristers, solicitors, court staff, journalists from television, radio and the press. And of course police, seven of whom are positioned in front of me. The only person not in there yet was the clown who wears the wig in the circus.

Focusing on MacIntyre, I make it clear what I think of him:

You are a mother's cunt. I hope you have twins as children and that they are both blind and keep bumping into each other. I hope you and your wife get riddled with AIDS. And I hope you get arthritis in both hands so you can't make any more statements, you grassing cunt. But I suppose it's nice to see that twelve years down the line you are still living off the back of me. I should really take that as a compliment.

Because we were in a court of law I think I took him by surprise. To me, he looked shocked but then seemed to get his self-assurance back and stared at me with a smug look on his face. A policewoman turned round and looked up at me in the dock.

'That is disgusting Jason. How can you say such horrible things to someone?'

I didn't give a fuck what she thought.

'Fuck off you slag. You'll probably have a Muslim hanging out the back of you later.'

She looked at me, very disapprovingly, and shook her head.

The Old Bill next to her joined in.

'You are just about to get sentenced. How can you talk like that?'

'I couldn't give a fuck.'

In comes the old chocolate fudge. He starts waffling on about how I am a disgrace to society; that it's not the first time and that I should have learnt my lesson. While he is talking I have my hands behind my back and a very sober expression on my boat. But when he puts his head down into his notes I turn to the journos to my right and smile and wink at them. They probably thought I wasn't all there, but, to me, body language is a big thing and I wanted them to know I accepted jail time as an occupational hazard.

I couldn't have cared less what the judge was saying. All I want to know is what I will be getting. Eventually, he comes to the sentencing. He tells me I will go to prison for two years and eight . . . . I thought he was going to say eight months, but what he actually says is 'an eight-year football ban'.

That morning I had told my neighbour Jeff Majors that I would thank the judge no matter what sentence I got. I didn't want them to think they had won; I wanted my body language to say I didn't care. So I smiled and said, 'Thank you your honour.'

It wasn't too bad. My starting point had been two years four months

160

for a guilty plea and although two years was out of all proportion for my offence it was still less than the guidelines I had been given. Mick the Plumber walked out with a fine and community service while Muggsy and John had a bus ride with me to look forward to. I can't remember how long they got but it was a lot less than me. Put it this way, I wouldn't even unpack.

Billy Matthews, Gary McGovern, Sean Fullicks, Kev and James Healy were just a few of those who came to see me off. To this day I really appreciate it. Sean still says to me, 'You're mental. I can't believe what you said to the Mongrel. As for thanking the judge, that's not normal.'

I smile and wink and say, 'It's not me. It's steak-and-kidney who lives in my head.'

30

Keeping Spirits Up

Although it was now back to prison I had the distinct advantage of being seven weeks into my sentence. The first couple of months inside are always the hardest simply because everyone takes time to adjust. But I had already gone through that period of adjustment – I normally adapt quickly to new situations anyway – so it made things that much easier.

Over the next few weeks and months more and more of our lads came through the door. Many had never been in jail before so I wanted to show them the ropes, help them get through it. Some of them had been sentenced the same day as me and so I would ask the jailer, 'Put him in the same cell as me. He's my mate.' The jailer did as I asked, which helped me get the lads prepared for what was to follow. The likes of Adam Rawlings, Tony Gunter, Sizey, Ian Cutler, Craig McGuire and Wally: I can honestly say they did Chelsea proud by getting their heads down and getting on with it. I said I'd do my best to get them a job. However, my focus was on Adam Rawlings because his girlfriend was pregnant, his granddad was ill and a close relative had been charged for the fight with Cardiff.

That first night back in the Scrubs everyone was held in the overnight cell before being allocated a cell on the wing. Everyone that is, apart from me: I got taken straight to my cell on C wing. I don't know how people knew when I was coming back but they just erupted. 'Well done Jase,' they cheered as they kicked the doors. It was because they had seen me on the TV news.

I got led into my cell and my old mucker Jeff Majors passed me a curry he had made through the window. As I tucked into the Ruby my padmate Manny asked if I was happy with the result. 'It's sweet. It will do. It is what it is.'

* * *

A few weeks had passed when Wally – a Chelsea mate who was sent down for Cardiff on the same day as me – told me he was getting a move to another nick. I was cleaning the landing when he walked up to me, obviously very excited.

'Jase, Jase they're shipping me out. I'm getting a move. I'm going to Ford. Where is it?'

'It's an open prison down Chichester way,' I told him.

When he had gone I thought there was a right good chance to have a laugh at Wall's expense. I went to the screws' office and got a general application form that covers everything and filled it out. I basically wrote that due to a clerical error Wally had been re-categorised and would be going to HMP Parkhurst. I waited for a couple of hours then slipped the form under his door, before carrying on with the cleaning. A bit later Wally came into my cell, obviously shattered.

'Jase, Jase. They're moving me.'

'I know that Wall. You told me. You're going to Ford.'

'No. They're moving me to Parkhurst. Where's Parkhurst?'

'That's the Isle of Wight, Wall.'

'How the fuck am I going to get there?'

'Don't worry, they'll take you,' I reassured him.

'How's my Caroline [his wife] going to get there?'

'It's easy Wall. She drives to Portsmouth and gets on the ferry.'

'She can't do that. I can't go there.'

'It ain't a fucking holiday, Wall. You are not picking your own destination. Believe it or not you are in prison.'

He carried on complaining. He looked a broken man. I pretended to be helpful.

'Go to the office and talk to the kangas about it,' I told him.

So he went to see the screw and the screw told him that he would be on the next bus to Parkhurst. Little did Wall know that I had the screw boxed-off.

I let Wally sweat it out for several hours before putting him out of his misery. Of course he called me every cunt under the sun and said he had been in bits about it. Eventually, knowing what I was like, he forgave me and found it funny.

* * *

Wormwood Scrubs wasn't a bad nick to do time in. In fact I would have been happy to have done my entire sentence there. I was in a good routine and was doing the job I wanted to do. But it doesn't work that way when you are behind the door: more and more people were coming into the Scrubs and it was time to be shipped out. So I was sent to Highpoint prison in Suffolk.

Highpoint was a sore nick. Lucky for me two of my pals were working in reception: Alan Hough and Mark Dickman. So I had a leg-up from day one. But there were more cunts in the place than I had ever come across in my life. Out-and-out scumbags. They weren't my kind of people. I am talking mainly about junkies who snorted Subitex, which comes in capsule form and is a substitute for heroin. They are given the capsule by the prison doctor and have to prove to him they have swallowed it. But they find ways round that: either by keeping it in the back of their throat or swallowing it and then sicking it back up. It is absolutely disgusting. When they get back to their cell they break up the capsule and snort what is inside or mix it with something and sell it.

So I wasn't sorry when I was moved on again, this time to Edmunds Hill prison, also in Suffolk. There were a few good lads in there – Lee, Cekic, Whyte, Mossy, Bow – but a lot of scumbag junkies too. Still, in the early days it was pretty comfortable. I got the landing cleaner's job again, which meant I could go the gym, and was therefore able to do my sentence my way. I even had the chance of a couple of wind-ups, which of course are my speciality.

I had the kitchen boxed off, so I used to get eggs, spices, powder and other bits from my pal who worked in there. They were all the little things I needed to make kettle curries in my cell. They could also be used for other purposes, like winding up my fellow cons.

There was this one kid. His name was Stephen Friend and it was his first time inside. He was a real straight runner if there ever was one and me and my mate, Lee Cekic, used to have a right laugh at his expense. This day I walk into Stephen's cell with a fairly large bag of Nikki Lauda.

'What's in the bag, Jason?' he asked.

'It's smack ain't it. I have just served everyone up with their gear.'

I tried to give him the Fleetwood Mac. He turned white as a sheet.

'No, no, no. I can't have that near me.'

'You need to lose a bit of pudding. All you ever do is eat cake and biscuits. Why don't you have a go on it?'

He looked at me in total amazement.

'I have never seen it.'

'Do us a favour. Just plug it up for me?'

'Nah, nah. I can't do that,' he spluttered.

I then go over to my mate Robert Patrick's cell, which is opposite Steven's. Ten minutes later Steven goes to use the phone and leaves his cell door open. I tell Robert to tell Steven that when we were banged up I had stashed the gear in his cell. So that night Robert shouts over to Steven, 'Jason has stashed the gear in your cell, Steven.'

The next morning when everyone gets unlocked to go to work, Steve's at the end of my bed.

'I haven't slept and I have had my cell upside down three times looking for it,' he says.

'Don't worry about it. You're mad. It's not even in there,' I assure him, in my most persuasive voice.

A few days later I walk into his cell with the brown bag well concealed in the pocket of my shorts. I march into his toilet and then walk out with the brown bag in my hand.

'Thanks for that, Steve. Everyone's climbing the wall for their gear. This lot will be gone today.'

'What do you mean?' he gulps.

'Thanks for stashing the gear.'

'I looked everywhere for that. Where was it?'

'Well I couldn't keep it in my cell. I would have got nicked.'

He was close to tears by this point. I kept the wind-up going for a few hours then came clean.

'It's only curry powder Steve. I use it to make curries in my kettle you nutter.'

Talking about food brings to mind another little incident in Edmonds Hill, which in its own way was almost as funny. In the nick a lot of people jump on the Muslim diet because they think the food is better. Not me, I would rather cook my own in my kettle.

In prison you come across a lot of snide Muslims. Sparkle was in that category, only a Muslim when he wanted to be. He broke every rule in the Koran, especially at Ramadan, when he would smoke, listen to music and watch television. I pulled him up daily about it but he would just laugh.

During the holy month of Ramadan the Muslims got their food in containers and a heated bag, as per their religion. So when we all went to the servery at around five the Muslims would be given their containers in a bag, which they then take back to their cells to eat at sunset. Everyone gets banged up at 6.30 p.m. and no one knows what they're doing behind their door.

Sparkle had been even worse than usual about breaking the rules so I had been pulling him up about it.

'You've been smoking, watching TV, listening to music. All sorts. Allah ain't gonna be happy with you mate.'

A short time later he asked me what was on the telly.

'Have a look at the paper in my cell,' I replied.

While he was reading the paper I put the clock in his cell forward an hour. Later that evening – it was half seven but he of course thought it was half eight – I shouted over to him, 'How was your grub Sparkle?'

'It was blinding mate.'

'Well Allah's not going to be very happy with you again,' I said

'What do you mean?'

'Well I put your clock forward an hour. It looks like you and Allah will fall out.'

'You can't do that to me, Jase.'

But he saw the funny side and admitted he had been hungry. It just shows that in a lot of cases the Muslim thing in prison is bollocks. So many of them break the rules you wonder what the point is.

But it's hardly surprising that so many cons pretend to be Muslim. Nowadays the prison system bends over backwards for them. In one prison I was in I decided to have my say. So I asked a kanga if I could speak to the No. 1 governor.

'Is it something I can help you with?' the screw asked.

'No. How many governors does this nick have? I don't want to speak to any other governor apart from the No. 1 governor,' I told him.

The next day, lo and behold, the No. 1 governor himself came to see me. Not hard because, after all, I was in prison.

'What seems to be the problem?' he asked.

'I'll tell you what the problem is. The other day we was given a Cadbury's Creme Egg for our pudding. What I'd like to mention is that everyone in the prison was given a Cadbury's Creme Egg as a pudding.'

'What's the problem with that?'

'I'll tell you the problem. It's Easter time and I'm a Christian. I'd like to know why the Muslims also got a Cadbury's Creme Egg when they're

Muslims, not Christians. When it comes to Ramadan I don't get a curry brought in from outside caterers like they do. So I'd like to know when this law's going to change because I'm being victimised.'

His response?

Let's put it this way. I think I had overstayed my welcome at that nick. I got shipped out a few days later.

* * *

So, barring the junkie scum, everything in Edmunds Hill was cushty: the job, my mates, the wind-ups. Until this day a new screw comes on the scene.

I had just come back from the gym and the new kanga was making himself busy. He was trying to stamp his authority on the place by disrupting us, which was completely unnecessary because up to that point everyone was just getting on with it, screws and cons. A few of us had a go at him, verbals only, but he was obviously worried enough about it to put it in the book, which security looked at daily, and anyone who has been inside knows that security runs the prisons.

The next thing I knew was being dawn raided. I was lying in my bed when a dozen screws and a governor come marching into my cell. The governor looks at me.

'You're going,' he said.

'Sweet,' I reply.

I was told to get some basics, which I did, and I was on my way. They also took Mossy and Lee Whyte. It was a classic screw's-word-against-ours. They had no evidence of any wrongdoing, and there was nothing on camera. But that has never stopped them. They put us in a sweat box (a prison van, for those of you who have never been in the nick) and whisked us off to Highpoint where they had a segregation unit. The Ritz it is not: there is no TV; you have to wear prison-issue clothes; you can only shower once every two days; phone calls every few days; and one sheet of writing paper a week.

In addition you have to see one of Highpoint's fifteen governors within twenty-four hours of being taken to the seg. Which is why I found myself in a governor's office with two screws behind me, a probation officer on my left and the mental-health worker to my right. The governor was sitting at a desk in front of a big photo of Her Majesty the Queen and without any further ado he got down to business.

167

'You know what you're here for.' It was more of a statement than a question.

'I ain't got a clue,' I responded.

'Intimidating an officer.'

'I don't know what you're talking about.'

'I have no alternative but to ship you out of this prison. There's no ifs and buts. You will be going.'

'Fantastic,' I told him and I meant it. I was trying to get over to him that Highpoint was a shithole and that there were many better nicks elsewhere.

'Do you have anything to say?' he asked.

I looked at him and then up at his wall.

'That's a lovely photo of the Queen. Could I have it for my cell?'

With that, I turned to the mental-health officer and smiled and winked at her. They knew I wasn't off my nut. I just wanted to have a laugh at their expense and to show they couldn't faze me. Never let the bastards get you down, as the saying goes.

I have to be charged within forty-eight hours for the alleged offence of intimidating a prison officer, either by that governor or one of his colleagues. But when they came to charge me it was outside the forty-eight-hour period and I had got the prison-law solicitor onto it very quickly. So no charges were ever laid against me.

Another few weeks passed and I was still down in the karaoke. By law a governor has to come and see you every day to ask if you are all right. This day I'd fucking had enough so I said to him: 'No as it happens, I ain't. You ain't charged me with anything. I have been down here a couple of months. What's fucking going on? You're taking me for a cunt. So I want to make a phone call to my prison-law solicitor.'

To cut a long story short, I ended up having a bit of a scream-up. The governor told me to calm down but I told him up his bollocks, there's no worse punishment than what I'm receiving, so he could go fuck himself and get me on the first bus out of his vile shithole.

Later that afternoon the senior officer comes to see me and says, 'I've had a word with one of my pals to see if they'll take you upstairs in Highpoint. I've told him your page 16 is good so you should fit back into the regime very quickly.'

I stewed on it for a day or two and eventually went back to a normal location, where, lucky for me, my good pal Tony Donovan, who I was in Edmond's Hill with, was on the same landing. So at least I had one good sensible face and pal around me.

31

If You Don't Shoot, You Don't Score

I think I am right in saying that after two-thirds of any football ban you have the right of appeal the banning order. So, six and a bit years after I got the ten-year ban on the conspiracy charges, I seized the opportunity with both hands. I called my QC, Michael Wolkind, who is one of the top briefs in England. I am still pals with Michael today and it was him, of course, who defended me when I got put away for conspiracy.

I felt I had nothing to lose. After all, it might give me the chance to go back and watch my team again. I could also have done without the headache of having to sign on at the police station before every home game or to hand in my passport every time Chelsea played abroad.

Eventually, we got a court date. But little did I know that it would be at the same place, Blackfriars Crown Court, where Nightmare and I had been tried and found guilty on the conspiracy charges. The case would also be heard by the same man, His Hon Judge the Hon Charles Byers (which, believe it or not, is his official 'style', according to Debrett's, the guidebook to the upper classes). I didn't know it was going to be the same judge or the same court. Nor did I consider whether being in the same court, before the same judge, would help or hinder my case. I didn't think I was going to win the appeal anyway.

I just thought I would give it a go. If you don't shoot, you don't score.

When I arrived at court there were a lot of people milling about and I presumed there must have been a big trial coming up after my short hearing. I entered court number one and once again came face to face with His Hon Judge the Hon Charles Byers, the man who had handed me a six-stretch for the BBC documentary.

'You can sit in the public gallery this time, Mr Marriner,' he said.

'That's very kind, your honour. It's nice to know that whatever happens I will be going home tonight.'

The prosecution kicked things off, arguing that the banning order should stay in place. They gave many reasons: I had written a book; I had featured in lots of other books; I had a DVD out; I was doing after-dinner talks; I had been spotted with other Chelsea Headhunters around the country; I had a website, from which they had printed extracts. The list went on and on but their bottom line was that I had become a legend and was cashing in on my notoriety.

Michael stood up and fought my corner to the best of his ability, countering every argument they put forward. I was asked to come forward and stand in the dock. It was only then that I realised that all the people standing outside were now in the public gallery. It was blatantly obvious they were journalists.

Judge Byers started to waffle on about when he had originally sentenced me. He noted that he had given me a twenty-year football ban but had reduced it to ten years, which is the maximum allowable under the law. He said that if he could have given me a twenty-year ban he would have been happy to start it from today and that there was no way my appeal would be granted.

When he finished speaking I turned to the pack of reporters who were frantically scribbling in their notebooks, and smiled.

Byers then asked the prosecution lawyer, a Mr Vodain, how much the costs were for the hearing.

'£600, your honour,' he replied.

'Blimey. I'm in the wrong game. I've only been in the court for twenty minutes,' I said.

'And how would you like to pay for your hearing Mr Marriner?' Judge Byers asked.

I looked at the journalists, pulled on my ear lobe and turned my head back to face Byers.

'But your honour, there's nothing wrong with my hearing,' I told him.

'Print that in your poxy paper,' I thought.

At this point Michael got back up and said to Byers: 'I am sure you will remember my client's humorous side, your honour. We will ask for time to pay.'

As you might have guessed the journalists didn't put my humour in their poxy papers. Instead they ran a story with the headline, 'Thug's Ten-Year Ban Stays.'

32

SO 19

Trouble (or Unlucky) is my middle name. Sooner or later something happens and there I am, right in the thick of it yet again. It was 2010, four days after my ten-year football ban had finished. Chelsea were playing West Ham at home and I decided to meet a few of the lads at the Seven Stars in North End Road.

So there we were outside the pub having some right good banter amongst ourselves when a Somalian family walked past. As we were laughing and joking one of them must have thought we were taking the piss out of them. So he turned round and said something to us, which, from his body language, I could tell wasn't very friendly.

Talk about being paranoid! No one was taking the piss. In fact we hadn't even noticed them. So we told them in no uncertain terms to fuck off. One of them started getting tricky, saying that they would phone the police. After verbals had been exchanged I ended up telling the geezer, 'Do what you fucking like. I'll wait here for them. I ain't going anywhere.'

Obviously being a match-day, there were a lot of cozzers about. But even so we didn't expect it to go any further, mainly because we had done fuck-all wrong. To our surprise, about twenty minutes later, they turned up. A van pulled up and eight Old Bill jumped out. It turned out that Mr and Mrs Somalia had made a complaint so the cozzers took it upon themselves to arrest me.

The lads I was with took the hump at the sight of me in handcuffs and there was a standoff with the officers who had arrested me. But I said to the lads, 'Leave it. No one's done anything wrong.' Things calmed down and I was taken to the nick where I was charged under the Public Order Act.

That charge gave the Old Bill the power to ban me from the surrounding areas and from football. Although it was not a football-related offence it had taken place on a match-day and in the vicinity of Stamford Bridge. Even I saw the funny side – just four days after serving a ten-year ban here I was getting another ban.

A year later I go to trial. While I am waiting to go into the kangaroo court I find out that the prosecution want to do a deal with me for the lesser charge of an offence under the Public Order Act, section four. I think they thought that because I didn't have a brief with me I would accept whatever they came up with.

Fuck that. I know the game as well as anyone.

I started laughing and asked them where their key witnesses, Mr and Mrs Somalia, were.

'They haven't turned up yet,' I was told.

Anyway, we get called into court where the prosecution ask for the case to be adjourned as the Somalians hadn't turned up. I saw my chance. I got to my feet and had my say.

'Well I managed to get here on time. The case has been going on for a year. This court is a mile and a half from where they live.'

I urged the court to hear the case right here and right now because, of course, I knew that without Mr and Mrs Somalia there was no evidence against me. The judge asked the prosecuting lawyer where he thought the Africans would be. But before he could answer I butted in. I couldn't resist it.

'Your honour, I think it's their signing-on day.'

What I really wanted to say was that they were illegal immigrants and that was why they hadn't turned up.

'Have you got a contact number for them?' the old chocolate fudge asked the prosecutor.

When it was confirmed there was a phone number he granted a short recess to allow the brief to bell them. Five minutes later we were back in court, at which point the brief announced that no one was answering the calls. The judge asked if I was willing to accept the section-four charge. I smiled but politely declined. With that the chocolate fudge said that in the absence of witnesses there was no case to answer.

I thanked the judge and walked out of the court with a broad grin on my face. I knew that I had accepted the lesser charge it would have meant a verdict of guilty and another football ban. That wasn't on. They had already succeeded in banning me for a year while I was waiting for the trial.

And it would have been yet another conviction for my CV.

* * *

After coming out for Cardiff I couldn't go to football, thanks to my ban. That didn't mean I stayed out of trouble, which always seems to find me. It was 2012. I had been out on the piss all day and, as you do, I had an argument with this herbert, who threatened to call the Old Bill.

'Go fuck your grandmother. Do what you wanna do,' I told him, quite reasonably.

I went home lagging drunk and thought no more of it. The next thing I knew I had the cozzers knocking on my front door. I ignored them so they went round to the front, and back, windows and shone this big torch right into my living room and my kitchen. I was so fucking drunk I just went to bed and let them get on with their banging, hammering and shouting.

Eventually, due to the din, I went to the window and opened it. I asked what they wanted and, can you believe it, it was me they were after. They said they wanted to speak to me about an incident. I told them I didn't know what they were talking about. I had nothing to say to them about anything.

'We think you are armed,' one of them said.

'Only with a wealth of knowledge. Now fuck off,' I replied.

But this was no joke. The next thing I knew I've got SO19, the firearms unit, surrounding my place. Not only that they had taped off the surrounding streets.

A standoff of about two hours followed. You'll have read about sieges in the papers or seen them in the movies. They are tense, cat-and-mouse affairs, with maximum psychological pressure being exerted by the massed ranks of Robocops outside. The man inside is gradually driven to breaking point by the mind games. Unable to take any more he either gives himself up, makes a break for it or starts shooting at the police.

Me? I tried to go to sleep.

To be fair, the fact that I was lagging drunk played its part, but I wasn't going to play their silly fucking games. If they wanted to stand outside for hours on end let them. I didn't give a fuck what they did. All I wanted to do was get my head down for a bit of a kip.

I eventually go outside and get arrested and am then taken to a police station. This gives them the chance to do a search of my house, during which they turn up a baseball bat, a hockey stick, knives, a hammer and tear gas. I eventually get charged with an offence under the Firearms Act for the tear gas. They also question me about the other 'weapons' but, as I would later testify in court, none of them are illegal.

While I was in the station this fat old pig came to my cell and asked if I was Jason Marriner.

'Are you a police officer?'

'Yes.'

'Then do your homework and don't ask stupid fucking questions,' I told her.

'I need you to come to the hatch in the door as I am re-arresting you.'

Seven hours down the line and now they want to charge me with a separate offence. What a liberty.

'Go fuck yourself. If you want to charge me you will have to come in and do it because I ain't getting off my comfortable blue mattress.'

I had already had my solicitor there and I had remained silent as normal. So I reminded them that as I was being charged with a separate offence I was entitled to make another call. I phoned my brief, who had already left the station, and told him that I didn't want to speak to the mongrels. He had a word with them and then we spoke again. He said my new charge was football-related as I hadn't informed the authorities of my change of address.

I just laughed. It was hardly the Great Train Robbery.

When I went to court, naturally I pleaded not guilty to both offences. I told the judge I had had a party one weekend and someone had obviously left the tear gas in my flat. The prosecution argued that the things I was likely to keep would be football-related, for example tear gas. I made the point that I had friends who had invited their friends, people that I didn't know, and maybe they had left the tear gas there.

The prosecuting barrister then brought up the other weapons, or, more accurately, what he classed as weapons. I quickly reminded the court of a number of facts: I had recently put up a picture on the wall using the hammer; me and my pals had been in the park playing baseball; the knives were not illegal unless you are carrying them on the street; and my mate's girlfriend had left her hockey stick there.

More to the point I had not been charged with possession with any of these 'weapons' so they didn't need to be mentioned. Then, when he asked me about my change of address, I asked him: 'Have you ever had a letter turn up late or go missing?'

I then looked at the judge and told him:

'I sent a letter your honour. It's not my fault that the postman didn't do his job properly and the football-banning authorities didn't receive it.'

Eventually, they wiped their mouths with the trivial matter of the letter, accepting that the postman had a bad day at the office. But the tear gas, given my form, was always going to be hard to get out of. I got a fine, community service and a year's probation.

The bloke in charge of community service was ex Old Bill but, to be fair, he was cushty. Let's put it this way: on my first day it took me eight hours to paint a door frame. Other people were working like dogs. He was suspicious of course but I tried to explain that we wanted to get the job just right. I ended up doing two days a week, instead of the standard one day, just to reduce the amount of weeks.

33

An Evening with . . .

Never in a million years did I ever imagine that I would end up doing a live show like *An Audience with Jason Marriner* or after-dinner talks. Fair enough, I made a DVD about my exploits but going out onto a stage and talking about myself, trying to make people laugh, is a whole new ball game. But I am so glad I did because I enjoy it.

You will have heard of Dave Courtney. Dave is a well-known south London villain, so respected that he organised the security for Ronnie Kray's funeral. Sometimes he is referred to in the press as 'the most feared man in Britain', while others describe him as the '*Yellow Pages* of the underworld'. Dave is also as funny as fuck and he has been doing an act for years. He, and others, said to me that I should get into it because I am funny and also have a lot of great stories to tell. So I started appearing as a guest on his shows and then I started to do my own shows. One thing led to another and I have done untold live performances up and down the country.

The first part of my act is normally me talking to the audience about the golden years of football violence, the courts, prison and the true facts behind the BBC documentary on me. Then I take forty-five minutes of questions. The four most common things I get asked are:

1. How did MacIntyre get onto you?
2. Who's the hardest firm you have ever come across?
3. Which firms do you rate?
4. When are they going to make a film about your life?

When I first started with the act I could feel my hands trembling. I don't think I am anything special and that made it harder. To this day I am a little embarrassed about it because people are paying their hard-earned cash to come and see me. I am so grateful to them and for that reason I try to give 100 per cent at every show. I want them to walk out thinking that was a really good night; that they got their money's worth.

I have of course had problems with the Old Bill. Many a time the police have stopped the show from going ahead. They threaten the owners of the venue, telling them they will lose their licence if it goes ahead. Maybe they would prefer it if I sold heroin to kids. Fuck knows. I have appeared all over Britain, including in Belfast, and also in Marbella. I have always had good audiences, with great people in them. I try to get the banter and audience participation going because, the way I look at it, it's their show not mine.

Sometimes I appear on my own, sometimes with other speakers, who have included some of the most interesting geezers you could ever meet. Take Howard Marks: middle-class background, brilliant at school, Oxford University graduate, drug-smuggler extraordinaire. He got twenty-five years in a tough American penitentiary for being, as one paper describes him, the 'most sophisticated drugs baron of all time'. I have known 'H' for twenty years and what a lovely fella he is; very mellow, good company, great sense of humour. When you are talking to him he just can't understand why you are not allowed to light up a spliff right there in the pub. I am not surprised either that his autobiography has sold over a million copies or that a film – *Mr Nice*, starring Rhys Ifans – was made about his life. Howard and I have done shows together and it is always a pleasure to share a stage with such an intelligent man. We call our shows *Mr Naughty, Mr Nice*.

I have also done loads of shows with Danny Dyer, star of the hit movie *The Football Factory*, in which he takes on the role of Tommy Johnson, a member of a Chelsea hooligan mob. As Danny is a close friend of mine I have put him on many shows with me. Of course we later did the documentary series *Real Football Factories* together and we get on really well. Danny is a West Ham fan, but has never been involved in football violence. He is a working-class lad who has done well for himself, a genuine, down-to-earth bloke I am fortunate to call a friend. In October 2013 he started in *EastEnders*, so good luck with that mate.

Danny is not the only showbiz pal I have made. I met Nick Miles and Dave Healey, at the opening of Howard Marks's wine bar in Leeds. Both of them were in *Emmerdale* where they played two out of the three brothers King. Nick is an Arsenal fan while Dave follows Rangers due to his family connections and still goes up to watch them. I stayed in touch with Dave and we became good friends. Someone else I got to know well is Frank Harper. He played 'Billy Bright' in *The Football Factory*, a florist/market trader who is also the leader of Chelsea's hooligan mob. They say the Bright character is based on me, given that my mum and my sister had a market stall selling flowers, and that I was also of course a leading Headhunter. But I've no idea how true that is. I am also doing a few shows now with the unit himself, Razor Ruddock. We call it *From the Pitch to the Terraces*. Trust me, it is one funny night.

Another good pal is the one and only Frederick 'Brown Bread Fred' Foreman. Freddie is a genuine legend, someone who has operated at the highest levels in the criminal underworld. He first came to public prominence when he got ten years for disposing of the body of Jack 'The Hat' McVitie, who was stabbed and killed by Reggie Kray in 1967. I don't understand what the problem was, after all undertakers get paid for disposing of bodies all the time!

I first met Fred in the Eighties. I was out on holiday in Fuengirola, where Freddie was on his 'Bromleys' due to his involvement in the 1983 Security Express blag in Shoreditch. He and his gang got away with £6 million, which at the time was the biggest heist in British history. While I was in Spain I got invited to a party at Ronnie Knight's villa, who, as it happened, was also on his Bromleys for the same job. It was the heyday of the Costa del Crime, that golden age before Britain had an extradition treaty with Spain, where faces from east and south London went to avoid the long arm of the law. It worked for a while but both Ronnie and Freddie were later convicted for Security Express and got long sentences.

It was a hell of a party. There was a band, a barbecue and as much drink as you wanted. Things must have got a bit out of hand as far as the other residents on the complex were concerned, because all of a sudden the lights went out and the music stopped. Someone, probably the caretaker, had turned off the electricity at the mains, no doubt after getting complaints from the other residents. It was the worst move he ever made because Freddie and a few of his henchmen went round and did him.

I knew who Freddie was and when I saw him for the first time I couldn't believe I was in his company. He spoke to me with such respect that I walked away thinking 'what a gentleman'. He was one of the most-feared gangsters in London, but he had spoken to a 17-year-old boy with such patience and respect. We have been friends ever since, meeting up regularly and speaking often on the phone. He is a loyal friend who has strong morals, a genuine top man and one of the nicest blokes ever.

34

Modern-Day Football

Former Chelsea chairman Ken Bates might be a controversial figure to some people but in my book he has always been fair-minded and straight. When I got nicked in 2000 he said in a match programme that he wouldn't take any action against me as I hadn't been convicted of anything. I thought, fair play to him, but that is the sort of bloke he has always been. In fact the club has never banned me from Stamford Bridge.

As far as the scarfers at Chelsea are concerned I don't have anything to say about them. I have been banned for so long that it would be difficult for me to give an opinion on what they are like these days. I am sure a certain element among them will always look down on me and the other lads because of what we have done. But I know for a fact that some of them are quite proud of the Headhunters and our reputation, because they have told me so.

So it is good that Chelsea has young lads coming through the system, as have most other clubs. They are known as the Chelsea Youth: Adam Rawlings, James Healey, Tony Gunter, Sizey and the rest of them. We call them the youth but they're not as young as you think. When they have it they will have it with other mobs' old schools; they don't just look for the opposition's youth. So fair play to them because it's the little wheels that make the big wheels go round.

Although it would be almost impossible to get to know the foreign legions who turn out for the club these days, I have become friendly with Chelsea players of the past, blokes from an ordinary English background like me. A lot of them are working-class kids from a council estate who have been lucky enough to live the dream. Take Kerry Dixon, who was born in Luton, and became a Chelsea legend thanks to almost a decade at the club and his incredible goal tally, which is close to two hundred. He was my hero during the Eighties and today I am lucky enough to call him a friend. We have done after-dinner speaking together and I found it funny when this promoter described one of our nights as 'Chelsea Legends'.

During the speeches Kerry will talk about what it was like when the Headhunters were being cunts on the terraces in the old days. In fact he and the rest of the players found it quite intimidating, especially because the crowds were usually very close to the pitch and could see exactly what was going on. It is great that he is still involved at the Bridge, doing hospitality and commentating on games for Chelsea TV. Jason Cundy is another former player who became a mate. He is on talkSPORT these days and he is just a very down-to-earth, nice fella. Other ex-Chelsea players who are now pals include David Lee, Mickey Thomas, Paul Canonville and Joe Allon. Mates who have played for other clubs include James Scowcroft, Geoff Horsfield, Paul Devlin and Paul Tait, while among my boxing pals are Robin Reid, Wayne Alcock, Darren Barker and Joe Egan.

What about Roman Abramovich? He has done great things for the club with his massive investment in players and facilities. I never thought I would ever see Chelsea winning the domestic double, let alone the Champions League of 2012 when, of course, we beat the Brussels sprouts, Bayern Munich, in their own backyard. Those were massive achievements and you can never take that away from the man. But to me he has spoiled it with all the sackings: we have had more managers than Bill Gates's companies. It goes back to the Mourinho dismissal in 2007 after he won us our first league championship in half a century. It wasn't just the trophies he won: the man obviously loved the club and should never have been shown the door.

Then look at the way Roberto Di Matteo was ditched after winning two trophies in his eight months at the club, including that Champions League final in Munich. Absolutely ridiculous. If he was the best caretaker manager of all time the worst surely has to be Rafa Benitez, who the vast majority of Chelsea fans hated after he cunted the life out of us in 2007 with his criticisms of our club. It was nothing to do with him being Liverpool manager. Let's hope Abramovich keeps faith with the Special One this time around even if in the short term the going gets tough. The fans love him and, let's face it, without us paying the wages there would be no club.

What do I think of football fans today? They're cunts, most of them.

There are still good working-class people among them but I am afraid that when your team becomes successful you breed a new band of supporters, otherwise known as the prawn-sandwich brigade. Then there are the foreigners. No I don't mean the players; I mean the fans, who now come from all over the world to watch Chelsea. The touts ain't interested in selling tickets to the average English fan, not when they can get double bubble from a Swede or the old Kitchen Sink. This used to be a game for the working man, but no more.

And I meant it when I used the phrase 'working man'. Look at the amount of women who go now. I don't have a problem with it but for them to go to every match? In my era, the terraces were full of lads, shoulder-to-shoulder; at a night match they would still be in their working clothes, straight off the building site. Now look at the stadiums to see how it has all changed.

Personally, I think the hooligan-banning regime suits the Premiership. It has meant they can get rid of those they see as not quite good enough for their swanky stadiums. After all we can't expect the suits to have their day out spoiled by having to mix with the oiks. I don't actually believe we are thugs, just people who are passionate about our clubs. But they are trying – and, I am sorry to say, succeeding – in driving us out of the game altogether.

35

Different Colours but We're All the Same

The only regret I have about football violence and my days on the terracing is that I never got a not guilty. To me it has been a way of growing up but they do say boys never really grow up. I am a firm believer that everyone on the scene, past and present, is passionate about one thing: his club, whatever club that might be, and my club happens to be Chelsea.

As far as my family is concerned it has probably not always been great for them. Because of all the publicity on television and in the papers my mum, who was a florist, got reporters coming up to her market stall and asking all sorts about me. Mum being Mum she just told them to fuck off. As far as my dad goes I have never really discussed football violence with him. I think he is proud of me and he loves me but is unhappy about the road I took in life and I don't suppose you can blame him for that. Nor would I ever blame them for anything I did; I had a good upbringing and the choices were mine and no one else's.

As I've got older and done the shows and met more and more good lads from all over the country, I have realised that we are all the same; we just happen to support a different club. In every firm you have different kinds of people: lunatics, funny people, quiet people, nice people. It just goes to show that no matter our differences we are all the same underneath.

In the early Eighties, Maggie Thatcher said that football violence is a cancerous disease and that we must stop it spreading. But we are now in the twenty-first century and this disease hasn't been cured and it isn't likely to be any time soon. I was just reading about an outbreak of serious disorder at a game. Was it in Manchester or London or Birmingham? No: it was in Atherstone, for fuck's sake. It was on 12 October 2013 during an FA Cup third-qualifying-round game between Atherstone Town and Barrow.

Atherstone (who come from darkest Warwickshire and have a stadium called, yes it's true, Sheepy Road) were playing at home. They were losing four-nil and as you can imagine their fans were not best pleased. They ran onto the pitch, invaded the away end, attacked the visiting fans, burnt a Barrow flag and even tried to get into the away dressing room to attack the opposition players.

What conclusion do I draw from this? I might start going to Atherstone! Only joking before the Old Bill get excited. Seriously, after working hard all week in a shit job for shit wages young men will want to fight. It doesn't matter whether you follow Man U or Chelsea or Atherstone Town. You will want a row. It's human nature and it ain't going to change any time soon. And once you are involved in the scene it takes you over. It's not so much a religion, more an addiction.

And it's an addiction you can't come off. The junkie has methadone to fall back on or he can call Frank (a helpline for junkies). Gamblers have got Gamblers Anonymous while alkies can call AA. But what has the bloke labelled as a football thug got? I'll tell you – he's got prison and that's his lot. Prison is meant to include rehabilitation but I'd like to know how being stuck behind a door is being rehabilitated. Football violence isn't a phase. It's a culture that is an addiction and you have to substitute something for that addiction, whether it's work or another sport.

For the most part we only fought with other like-minded people even though the media portrayed us as scum. If they think that labels like that upset us or stop us from having fun they couldn't be further from the truth. A football mob will only go looking for the opposition and we won't just bully anyone off the street. I have never attacked a scarfer and neither have my Chelsea pals.

I have never claimed to be hardest man around. I was just a game lad who would go and enjoy himself with pals who felt the same way. I have been a category-C hooligan, with a very high profile, for many years but things have changed for me now. Enough is enough and I have finally managed to cast aside my addiction and to settle down. Although I did my time inside without any problem a day behind the door is still a day too long. I don't want to be a hard man in prison. I want to be out in the fresh air, earning a crust.

That is especially true when you have a beautiful fiancée like Steph, who I have been with for a few years now. Behind every good man is a good woman and I've got that woman now. We met after one of my shows. She knew nothing about me or my show. We have a lovely little boy together, Frankie. She has never really understood the scene but I just tell her she doesn't need to understand it because those days are behind me.

My priority now is to make a better life for Steph, Frankie and me. My business as a tyre dealer disappeared – and my chance to become financially secure – when I went inside in 2000. So now I need to look around for something else to make a living at, in addition to the act. I have always been a market trader even when I had the shop and I have gone back to that line of business. It is something I am good at, having the gift of the gab, and being a bit of a character.

The markets I worked were for locals, not your Petticoat Lanes and the like, which are strictly for tourists. I have loads of contacts and people are always phoning up looking to do a bit of business, selling this and buying that. Me and my pal, Spencer Jones, do quite a bit of graft together. Other market traders have contacts too and I tap into that resource. I even went out to China a few times when I was younger to import stuff and now that I am off my licence I intend to go back there and to do a bit of business.

The problem is that the game has got a lot harder due to the recession and there are now very few old-school market traders left. There are too many people out there prepared to get up and work for a bowl of rice, doing their level best to undercut you. But I like to graft and I am not afraid to take a risk so we will see how it goes.

They tell me I wasn't a bad footballer. That I could have played at a higher level. But I came up against a few professionals in pre-season friendlies and it's only when you are on the same pitch that you realise they really are in a league of their own. You make your own luck in life and obviously I chose the wrong path.

That said, since I've been in the public eye I have played in a few celebrity charity matches, with the likes of Ralph Little, Geoff Frazier, Justin Edinburgh, Jimmy Carter, Geoff Horsfield, Paul Devlin and Paul Tait. It's nice to do something I enjoy for a good cause. Talking about charity, I am an ambassador for the Amelia-Mae Foundation. It was set up in memory of a little girl who, tragically, died of cancer at the age of just two.

One day you might even see my life story on the big screen. I have had meetings with Jonathan Sothcott, who is renowned for his crime and horror movies, such as *Vendetta, Devil's Playground, We Still Kill the Old Way* and *The Fall of the Essex Boys*. He is the best young producer in the business, a man with his finger on the pulse. We'll see.

In the meantime you will see me in a film, *Mob-Handed*, in which my character is out to kill paedophiles. I am happy to play this role because let's face it no one likes a 'bacon'. You may also have caught the Channel 5 documentary, *Hooligans and Proud*, which was televised in 2014, just three days before the World Cup in Brazil kicked off. The first I heard about it was when the production company phoned me to say they were working on a documentary about football hooligans and hardcore football fans. They were currently speaking to 'some of the big hooligans from back in the day' and also wanted to find out 'what it's like being a youth today. We would love to talk you,' they said.

That's how it started. I then spoke to a woman from the company, who went into more detail about what the programme was about. I interrupted her.

'Let me stop you there. How much?'

'Oh, we don't pay anyone.'

'How do you pay your British Gas bill?' I asked.

'What do you mean?'

'I'd like to know who pays your bills.'

'I do,' she said.

'Who do you think pays mine? If I'm with you and I'm not getting paid I can't earn money.'

She told me it was their policy that no one got paid to take part in documentaries.

'That's no problem. I have a similar policy. If I don't get paid, I don't work. Thanks for this conversation. We'll leave it at that.'

She asked if she could take my number, which I gave her. Some time down the line I had another call from her.

'Hi Jason. It's Mel from Channel 5.'

'Hi Mel. Have you changed your policy yet?'

'I'm sure we can come to some sort of arrangement.'

She kept going on about how good this documentary would be and what would come off the back of it.

'If I want to go on TV I'll go on *Crackerjack*. By the way, I've shaken hands on a film deal, I've got a new book coming out and my DVD is still selling well. I don't think that your documentary on Channel 5 will make much difference to my lifestyle.'

After a long discussion about money I decided that I would, after all, be the voice of reason although at that point I had no idea about who else was going to be on it or what credibility they would have among lads in the FV scene. I didn't like the title they chose for it, *Hooligans and Proud*, as I made clear to Channel 5. Why did I do it? I had a few good reasons.

To make money.

To plug the film about my life.

To plug this book you are reading.

To make it clear I am no longer involved in the scene and that I have well and truly moved on.

That was good enough for me. I can't help what other people said in the documentary, or how they came across, and, to be honest, I watched a lot of it under a quilt I was cringing so much. But I tried to be as straightforward as possible and at the end of the day that's all you can do.

36

In This Land, Every Little Bit of Grass Gets Cut

I get asked about MacIntyre all the time. I tell people, all the time he lives in my head rent free I ain't getting a pound note. To me, he's yesterday's fish-and-chip wrapper; he's old news.

He obviously had to be careful after what happened to me. According to him, after I went down he got death and kidnapping threats, had his car smashed up and was forced to move house many times. He managed to stay one step ahead.

Until, that is, 18 June 2009.

MacIntyre and his wife were out having a drink in the Cloud 9 wine bar in East Molesey, Surrey. According to him his wife was due to have a scan for a brain tumour and they were discussing her hospital appointment when a group of men, who had been eyeballing them, came over to his table. MacIntyre would later tell a court that the man in front said something like, 'You grass, you snitch; you put my pal Jason in jail.'

At this point, again according to MacIntyre, his wife became upset and went to the toilet and that shortly thereafter he followed her. He said that he made a request to a group of lads in the toilet: 'Give me a hard time if you want, but my wife's got a brain tumour.' MacIntyre was then asked by a woman why the men were shouting at him and put it to him it was because he had 'put someone in jail'. She then said, 'Well then you deserve it then don't you?'

MacIntyre and his wife decided to leave the bar but were followed by the men who had previously confronted them. One of the men said, 'You bastard I'm going to have you,' and at that point MacIntyre was knocked to the ground and set upon. According to his wife, who would also give evidence in court, the gang of men descended on her husband like 'a pack of wolves'.

She went on: 'It was a sea of people and while they were kicking him they kept saying, "Get him. This is for Jason." The men who attacked my husband were going to kill him.'

When I heard about what happened I found it quite funny, but I wondered what lies would come out in court. If he was on *Countdown* I would bet my bottom dollar that he wouldn't be able to spell the word truth.

The Old Bill nicked twelve people for the assault and during questioning it became clear that they were only interested in putting one Jason Marriner in the frame. Of course it had nothing to do with me. I was later gutted to hear that my old pal James Wild got two-and-half-years for harming a witness and assault occasioning actual bodily harm in connection with the Cloud 9 incident. He is a good lad and that is far too long for doing something that in my eyes MacIntyre had coming to him.

As they do say: 'In this land, every little bit of grass gets cut.'

Acknowledgements

Aaron Keppel, Aaron Smith, Abley Diop, Adam Budworth, Adam Fisher, Adam Kidson, Aitken, Al Kelly, Alan Ash, Alan Cooley, Alan Foskit, Alan Hopping, Alan McCaffrey, Alan Paramasivan, Alzi Paramasivan, Alan Pearce, Alan Reid, Ale Scotti, Alfie Summers, Alfie Summers Jr., Andrew Burke, Andrew Darby, Andrew Harper, Andrew Heywood, Andy Barnet, Andy Cruikshank, Andy Bedwood, Andy Frain, Andy Garner, Andy Gardner, Andy Harris, Andy Hills, Andy Linton, Andy Turner, Anthony Hillsted, Anthony Jones, Army, Aruhn Maharajh, Ashley Hayes, Barry Coffey, Barry Costa, Barry Esden, Barry Nuttall, Basher, Battersea Bill, Beau Courtney, Ben Usher, Billy Brown, Billy Chamberlain, Billy Collicot, Billy Fisk, Billy Holiday, Billy Hussain, Billy M, Billy Payne, Billy Steadman, Billy Whiteley, Blackpool Bennett, Blucky, Blue, Boatsy, Bob Anderson, Bob Chamberlain, Bob Furber, Bob Holiday, Bobby Keane, Bobby Tompkins, Bobby Watson, Bonny, Bonny Dave, Bonzo, Bose, Boz, Brains, Brendan McGirr, Brian Fullocks, Brian Furlong, Brian Gowers, Brian Gray, Brian Hall, Brian Houshby, Brian Tuff, Brian Wright, Brownie, Brummie Dave, Budgie, Bully, Buster Bloodvessel, Bruce Peak, Bubs Skully, Busby, Butch Alboni, Calvin Ewing, Cammy, Campo, Carlos, Carl Beresford, Carl Hammond, Carl Stenhouse, Carl Smith, Carlo Darlington, Carlton Leach, Cass Pennant, Chappy, Charlie Bronson, Charlie Summers, Chris Collins, Chris from Kilburn, Chris Griffiths, Chris Harwood, Chris Kempton, Chris Kidd, Chris Radwell, Chris the Greek, Chris Henderson, Chris O'Neill, Chris Whalley, Chonker, Chunker, Cliff Summers, Clive James, Cloudy, Cockney Tony, Cola, Colin Bell, Colin Gault, Colin Hannah, Colin Prior, Colin Barrett, Colin Reno, Colin Salmon, Craig Bonsall, Craig Crook, Craig Daley, Cutler, Daisy, Dale Thomasson, Damian McSorley, Daniel Beam, Daniel Twin, Danny Agnew, Danny Godfrey, Danny James, Danny Taylor, Danny Young, Darren Alboni, Darren Barker, Darren Barnwell, Darren Brewer, Darren Crewe, Darren Kerr, Darren Harman, Darren Ormiston, Darren Rowe, Dave Brown, Dave Casselars, Dave CFC UK, Dave Courtney, Dave Cox, Dave Cruickshank, Dave Dunne, Dave East, Dave Martins, Dave MacPherson, Dave Nye, Dave Paget, Dave Picknall, Dave Powell, Dave Sim, Dave Wallis, Dave Whitewick, Davey Carrick, Davey Duke, Davey Gilmore, Davey Mason, Dean Brewer, Dean Cox, Dean Hillier, Dean Lingham, Dean Russell, Dean Scott, Dean White, Del Goody, Dennis Shail, Dennis Flemming, Dennis Houlihan, Dennis Sheridan, Dessie O'Flynn, Dickie Parrot, Digger, Dinksy, Dipps, Disco, Dixie Hobson, Don the Gas, Donk, Duck, Eddie Barnes, Eddie Collis, Eddie Crispin, Eddie from Ulster, Eddie Tang, Eddie Wilds, Everton, Eoin McSorley, Fitz, Flynnie, Ford Davey, Fred Wilson, Frankie Fullbrook, Gappy, Gary Alleway, Gary Baker, Gary Bradley, Gary Brown, Gary Brunning, Gary Cambridge, Gary Cooper, Gary Ewing, Gary Gibbons, Gary Glazier, Gary Gurson, Gary Humphreys, Gary

Jenkins, Gary Long, Gary Maguire, Gary Mills, Gary Sumpter, Gary Tompkins, Gary Winslade, Giles, Gilly Shaw, Ginger Bob, Glen Hall, Graham Stack, Graham White, Grant Griffin, Graham Moore, Graham Mews, Graham Payne, Graham Russell, Greg Myers, Guy Hammond, Hanif, Harry Hogg, Harry Holland, Harry Robertson, Harry White, Harry (whine bar), Hayden Bowers, Helen Leadbetter, Henry Doe, Hickey, Hoody, Howard Marks, Huw Jones, Ian Drummond, Ian Duncan, Ian Freeman, Ian Hannah, Ian Holloway, Ian Kiernan, Ian McLean, Ian Sim, Ian Thompson, Ian Tovey, Imad, Ivan Collier, Jack Bravado, Jack Russell, James Bavin, James Cooley, James Ince, James Keye, James Kielty, James Saunders, Jamie King, Jamie Osborne, Jamie Robertson, Jamie Walford, Jamie Smith, James Wilde, Jason Collins, Jason Fenton, Jason Howells, Jason Hyland, Jason Scott, Jason Solomon, Jason Watson, Jason Weeks, Jay Davis, Jay Kelly, Jay Usher, Jay Willis, Jed Chamberlain, Jeff Battersby, Jeff Chelton, Jeff Scafarde, Jeff Sharp, Jeremy Richardson, Jerry Edmonds, Jimmy Keane, Jimmy Smith, Jimmy Stockin, Jim Stradlin, Jimmy Summers, Jimmy White, Jimmy Wright, Joe Butts, Joe Dowling, Joe Smith, Joe Slater, Joey Pyle, Joey Pyle Jr., John Anslow, John Calender, John Duke, John D'Urso, John Heather, John Holland, John Hollifield, John Jo O'Neill, John Kelly, John Laverick, John Leftley, John Mapletoff, John McNeil, John Mortimer, Johno, John Pidgely, John Wigmore, John Wilson, Johnny Helps, Johnny Sawyer, Johnny Sawyer Jr., John Wakeling, John Wallis, Johnny Blisset, Johnny Frankham, Johnny Matthews, Johnny Smith, Julian Classey, Justin Hughes, Justin Merrit, Keith Herman, Kelly, Ken Gilmour, Kenny Goodwin, Kevin Baker, Kevin Bushnell, Kevin Challenger, Kevin Cressey, Kevin Faithful, Kevin Gadsby, Kevin Glarvey, Kevin Houlihan, Kev Lanigan, Kev Maskell, Kev Sweeney, Kev Wesley, Kilburn John, Kingsley, Kristian Warby, Luckan Sinclair, Lance Hargreen, Lee Booter, Lee Colvin, Lee Devins, Lee Hillier, Lee Kidd, Lee Kerr, Lee Jackson, Lee Orme, Lee Payne, Lee Scott, Lee Spence, Lee Waite, Lee Whitelock, Lenny Hagland, Lenny Pidgely, Les Brum, Les Strong, Les Winslade, Liam Galvin, Lipsey, Little Tommy, Lol Aherne, Louis Williams, Maggy, Mal Vango, Malcolm Allen, Malcolm Carle, Manny, Marc Abrey, Marcus Fuller, Mark Abley, Mark Alleway, Mark Andrews, Mark Bamford, Mark Beam, Mark Bennett, Mark Campbell, Mark Carter, Mark Dane, Mark Dimbleby, Mark Drummond, Mark Fish, Mark Gregor, Mark Hickmott, Mark Hunt, Mark C, Mark Lord, Mark Marsla, Mark Monks, Mark Osbourne, Mark Parsons, Mark Peak, Mark Quigley, Mark Silbury, Mark Ward, Mark Wilson, Mark Wotton, Mark Wright, Martin Bats, Martin Denslow, Martin Steadman, Martin Ward, Martin Willis, Matty Clear, Matty Dormer, Matty Green, Matty Gould, Matty Morris, Matty Osbury, Matty Peak, Matty Robson, Matty Shadbolt, Matty Wigmore, Max Free, Max Scotti, Meady, Martin Denslow, Martin Fisher, Martin King, Martin Travis, Martin Ward, Max Free, Mensi, Michael Penny, Michael Wolkind QC, Mick Berry, Mick Collins, Mick Gadsby, Mick Maguire, Mick McSweeney, Mick the Badge, Mickey Cavanagh, Mickey Forrest, Mickey Gray, Mickey Hemmings, Mike Bish, Miles Cruickshank, Miles Saward, Millwall John, Mugsy, Murdo, Muzza, Nathan Twin, Nathan Wharf, Neil Carvey, Neil Fearnley, Neil Fisher, Neil Lucas, Neil Holland, Neil Phillips, Neil Watkins, Neil Wright, Nicky Hills, Nick Godfrey, Nick Owen, Nicky Penny, Nick Travis, Nigel Hobson, Nigel Smith, Nigel Venus, Noel Barrington, Norman Parker, Noski, Ollie Crompton, Olli Moeni, Paddington, Paddy Forrest, Palmer, Para Paul, Pascal, Pat Doland, Paul Atkinson (Rampton), Paul Blackmore, Paul Brooker, Paul Carney, Paul Coles, Paul Costa, Paul Cushion, Paul Dane, Paul Dowsit, Paul Gowans, Paul Hardy, Paul Keenan, Paul Levingstone,

Paul Manvelle, Paul Maguire, Paul O'Donovan, Paul Reid, Paul Riley, Paul Scarborough, Paul Sharp, Paul Tait, Paul Walsby, Paul Winter, Perky, Pete Summers, Peter Brown, Peter Lynch, Peter MacBeth, Peter Russell, Peter Volks, Peter White, Phil Hall, Paul Papaelias, Phil Riley, Philip Shields, Pieman, PJ, Porky, Pops, Rab, Ralphy, Ray Atkinson, Raymond Hill, Ray Harris, Razor Ruddock, Reza Moeni, Rhys Hefford, Richard Evans, Richard Linton, Richard Saxford, Richard Stringer, Ricky Ewing, Ricky Graves, Ricky McNamara, Ricky Steadman, Rob Allen, Robert Hoffman, Rob Honeyball, Rob Kiernan, Rob Ratcliffe, Rob Sumpter, Rob Sylvester, Robert Songhurst, Rocka, Rocky Alboni, Rodney Croney, Roger Crunchy, Rog Fabharwal, Roland Terry, Rolesy, Rolls, Roly, Romford Lee, Ronnie Borg, Ronnie Herbert, Rory Quigley, Roy Page, Roy Shaw, Russell McFadden, Russell Weeks, Sam Hickmott, Scatty, Scott Green, Sean Birch, Sean Keating, Shaun Baker, Shaun Bowman, Shaun Fullocks, Shaun Kidson, Shannon, Snide Sid, Silent Jason, Simon Bennett, Simon Brown, Simon Lawley, Simon Williams, Skeeny, Skippy, Skitsy, Sonny Ayinde, Spats, Spencer Allen, Spencer Jones, Spencer Willmott, Spider, Stacky, Steffan Bauldoff, Stephen Burke, Steptoe, Steve Alboni, Steve Blackmore, Steve Bradley, Steve Choules, Steve Clarke, Steve Clayson, Steve Collis, Steve Dunne, Steve Flatman, Steve Fogarty, Steve Gilmartin, Steve Healey, Steve Humphries, Steve Hyland, Steve Keane, Steve King, Steve MacPherson, Steve Nuttall, Steve Nye, Steve Parker, Steve Payne, Steve Proctor, Steve Reno, Steve Skully, Steve Taylor, Steve Thomas, Stuart Glass, Stuart Holloway, Stuart Monks, Stuart Shooter, Suitcase Eddie, Swiggy, Syksey, Tel Gallacher, Terry Butts, Terry Curtis, Terry Heather, Terry 'Tess' Mann, Terry Mann, Terry Newman, Terry Parks, Terry Turbo, Tim Rice, Timmy Lyons, Tom Furber, Tom O'Gorman, Tommy Capliss, Tommy Doyle, Tommy Keane, Tommy Tobin, Tommy Williams, Tonto, Tony Atkinson, Tony Covelle, Tony Freeman, Tony Harris, Tony Ludby, Tony King, Tony Murphy, Tony Newman, Tony Noland, Trav, Trigger, Troddy, Tuse, UK, Untold, Vaughn Jackson, Vince Drake, Vince Stapleton, Vince Stapleton Jr., Vince O'Flaherty, Vinny Hillier, Vinny Lynch, Wally Stockin, Walsby, Warren Glass, Warren Jenkins, Will Browning, Will Mason, Willy Reid, Winston, Yeti, Yoksi, Ziggy, Zorro.

R.I.P. Tim Rice, Aruhn Maharajh, Paul H. Hopping, Nicky Olpin, Steve Paget, Paul Treherne, Alan Glazier, Sid Rabbets, Ray Kennet, Ricky Alboni, Micky Greenaway, Barry Johnston, Simon Gillard, Mark Ash, Leslie Costa, Linda Costa, Kath Scott, Doddy, Dane Greensword, 'Chubby' Chris Henderson, Ernie Clancy, Darren Crewe, Jointy, Little Tommy, Fat Pat.

If I have forgotten anyone, please accept my apologies.